Michael Hogben's

101
ANTIQUES
OF THE FUTURE

Michael Hogben's

101
ANTIQUES
OF THE FUTURE

NEW HOLLAND

First published in 2007 by New Holland Publishers
London • Cape Town • Sydney • Auckland
www.newhollandpublishers.com

Garfield House, 86–88 Edgware Road, London, W2 2EA, United Kingdom
80 McKenzie Street, Cape Town, 8001, South Africa
14 Aquatic Drive, Frenchs Forest, NSW 2086, Australia
218 Lake Road, Northcote, Auckland, New Zealand

ISBN 978 1 84537 733 5

Although the publishers have made every effort to ensure that information contained in this
book was meticulously researched and correct at the time of going to press, they accept no
responsibility for any inaccuracies, loss, injury or inconvenience sustained by any person
using this book as reference.

Editorial Director: Jo Hemmings
Senior Editors: Steffanie Brown, Naomi Waters
Editor: Fiona Screen
Assistant Editor: Giselle Osborne
Designer: Alan Marshall
Production: Joan Woodroffe

Reproduction by Pica Digital Pte Ltd, Singapore
Printed and bound in Singapore by Star Standard Industries Pte Ltd.

DEDICATION: FOR MY TWO FAVOURITE ANTIQUES, BOTH FROM THE ART DECO PERIOD,
MY MUM AND DAD.

Picture Credits:
Front cover: A selection of 1970s furniture (top left); a selection of fishing lures (top centre);
A Clarice Cliff plate in the Autumn pattern and candlesticks in the Latona and Honolulu
patterns (top right); jade and amber necklace (bottom left); Charles and Ray Eames's iconic
Lounge Chairs (bottom centre); punk rock memorabilia album covers and singles (bottom
right).
Back flap: The author examining a selection of British marine paintings.
Spine: A doll replica of Geri Halliwell, also known as Ginger Spice, member of the 1990s
band The Spice Girls.
Back cover: A mobile telephone from 1987 surrounded by a selection of phone cards from
the 1980s and '90s (left); a selection of buttons from the 1920s (centre); assorted galvanised
watering cans.
Page 2: A selection of Festival of Britain medals (top left); enamel sign for St Julien Tobacco
(top right); cruet sets from the 1950s (bottom left); stainless steel kitchenware (bottom right).
Page 5: A selection of Troika pottery.
Pages 6-7: From left: An Asprey mantle clock stands alongside a pocket watch; a selection
of Carnival glass pieces; a Stuart Devlin silver-and-gilt limited-edition egg; a selection of
handbags from the 1950s.

Contents

Introduction

Collecting antiques has been a life-long passion for me, and the excitement and pleasure that it produces never subsides. Since having been an art dealer for five years and an auctioneer for over fifteen, I have personally sold over 15 million pounds worth of antiques, and over two million lots have passed through my hands.

Some of the most fascinating paths to follow for collectors are those that lie deep-rooted in the memory. The urge to accumulate objects from the past can lead to the formation of an immensely pleasurable collection, which can also – with a bit of luck and skill – be accompanied by a considerable financial reward.

Nearly everyone has, or can develop, an eye for some nostalgic item from the past. The urge to collect may come about in a number of random ways: all of a sudden you realise that you have just bought your third piece of Clarice Cliff, or maybe you have long been gathereing items connected with the area in which you grew up. Perhaps you are a fanatical gardener and have grown to admire the antique items that add such charm to that shady corners of your garden. Or maybe the implements used in kitchens past have caught your eye, especially if you are a promising chef. Chances are that an existing hobby or long-held interest is the stimulus for your collection.

Once you have made a decision as to what to collect, the field you have chosen will no doubt open up plentiful collecting possibilities, and you may have to whittle down your criteria even further. Should you only collect items in top condition? Should you limit yourself to the earliest examples? Perhaps only items of a certain colour or size catch your eye. The choice and the fun of collecting are entirely yours, and you can be certain that you'll always feel a sense of achievement from collecting your unique assortment of items.

Although the reasons for investing in antiques are abundant – enthusiasm for or enjoyment of a particular object, or to remind yourself of days gone by – one thing is for certain: you will want your antiques to represent a good financial investment. Investing in antiques can be similar to investing in the stock market in that the market will always have its highs and lows. Knowing when to invest, what to invest in and how much you should pay are all crucial factors for any prospective collector.

With the lure of antiques and collecting showing no sign of slowing down, I have decided to share my 25 years of experience with you and offer you some tips on which items I believe will be good future investments – and hopefully the subjects of enjoyable and interesting collects as well. In this book I have chosen 101 items which I strongly believe are destined to become the 'antiques of the future', meaning that they will, some time soon, become more valuable – and thus more collectable – than they are now. Furthermore, I believe that the items I have chosen currently represent a good buying opportunity: they are affordable at the moment, but may not remain so in the near future. I have chosen a wide range of items, from furniture to ceramics, and from

jewellery to postcards, in the hope that one or more of these items will spark your interest, and will lead you to develop a passion for whatever you have chosen to collect.

For each of the 101 items listed I have given important background information, including the object's history; information about the company or factory in which it was made and its designer(s); and a general description of its physical characteristics. Also included for each item is a list of 'items to look out for'; each item on this list has been chosen for its particularly good investment value, its relative rarity or desirability, or simply its beauty. A rough guide to what you should expect to pay for these items is also given. Finally, it is my pleasure to share with you my 'top tips' on finding, buying and maintaining each featured item so that it retains its value and integrity for as long as you own it.

It is my hope that at least one – hopefully more! – of the items in this book will catch your eye and inspire you to begin a collection that will bring you much joy as well as, should you decide to sell it on, financial reward.

These are the antiques of the future, so get in there now, while the going's good!

Starting a Collection

There are some basic rules that any collector, whether established or novice, should follow. Some of these may seem obvious, but I think

ABOVE: A selection of brass trench-art pieces from World War I.
OPPOSITE: A doll modelled after Geri Halliwell, also known as Ginger Spice from the 1990s band The Spice Girls.

they are worth mentioning lest you get caught up in the excitement of a sale and forget your common sense!

Do your research

Once you have chosen a subject to collect, one of the best investments you will make will be reference books, magazines and articles on your chosen subject. Particularly useful magazine titles include *Antiques and Collectibles*, *Collect It* and *Antiques Info*; otherwise you could skim through *Miller's Antiques Price Guide* or *Miller's Collectible Price Guide* to familiarise yourself with the characteristics and pricing of various items. These reference materials will help you to educate yourself on what you are about to collect, and we all know how important an education is.

In addition, many libraries have an 'antiques and collectors' reference section, so it may be an idea to pop down to your local library. London's Victoria and Albert Museum, for example, has one of the largest accessible collections of books on antiques in the country, and is thus definitely worth a visit. (For a

ABOVE: Antiques fairs are great places to learn more about a subject and to pick up a bargain.

list of recommended reading materials see page 124.)

You should also keep your eyes and ears open for collectors' clubs and exhibitions relating to your chosen subject. The knowledge you will attain is bound to enhance the pleasure to be gained from your collection. Furthermore, this is a good way to meet other collectors with common interests, and who may have items from their collection that they wish to sell – an easy way to expand your own collection! Conversely, should you decide that you wish to sell an item from your collection on (perhaps because you want to realise a portion of your financial investment, or perhaps to make space for the display of a new addition to your collection), you may find that you have a buyer right under your nose!

Joining a collectors' club will also allow you to keep abreast of current trends in the subject that you are collecting, which can be very useful in terms of knowing the value of what you own.

Buying and selling your collection

Antiques fairs and car boot sales

Antiques fairs and car boot sales are excellent places at which to familiarise yourself with the antiques trade as a whole. Car boot sales in particular are a fantastic and often underrated way to pick up a bargain buy. They are also a great place to sell your own stuff, especially if you want to get rid of a lot of items quickly. Try your local school, church or community centre's notice board for information on when and where local car boot sales are being held.

The Internet

The Internet is a great place to get an idea of what an object might be worth, making it a good starting point for beginning any collection. The famous auction site, eBay, is a fantastic place to look, as you can get a true sense of an item's value through the bidding process. You might also have a look at the websites of some of the more famous auction houses, such as Christies and Sotheby's. You can even check their recent auctions online to see how much money an item is selling or has sold for. And then, of course, you can use these sites to buy and sell your own items.

Auction houses

Should you decide to sell a few items from your collection, an auction room is an excellent place to do this. Like all businesses, auction houses have to make a profit to survive, and they do this is by charging the vendor (the seller) a commission charge; the buyer is charged a buyer's premium.

Commission charges vary from a staggering 25 percent to a negotiable commission-free deal. Most auction rooms charge a 15 percent (plus VAT) commission on items worth less than £1,000. For items with a higher value than £1,000, the commission rate usually becomes negotiable, depending on the reserve. If you have many items that you wish to sell, it is always worth negotiating with an auction house. For instance, if you have a complete house's contents to be auctioned, chances are that the auction house will negotiate a competitive commission rate, sometimes as low as five percent.

Auction houses will also charge an insurance fee (normally two percent), transport and illustration charge on top of their commission. This is all negotiable, but make sure you know how much you are going to be charged before you put your goods into the auction sale.

In my opinion it is always worth consulting two salerooms to find out where you will get the best deal on the commission rate. If you have a specialist item, I would recommend that you find an auction room that produces a nice glossy catalogue with illustrations. While London is known for its major salerooms, in today's market there are numerous smaller salerooms that now offer a similar service, sometimes at a more competitive rate. (See page 121 for a listing of auction houses that I think offer a competitive, professional and comprehensive service).

Damage and restoration

This is a subject worth knowing a bit about, as virtually every collector of older items is bound to encounter damaged or restored examples. In fact, I think it is safe to assume that fewer than 10 percent of all objects bought and sold in the vintage and antiques trades can be considered in perfect condition. Regrettably, no amount of careful handling or protection can prevent the occurence of damage; it is just a fact of life that the process of natural decay and the elements make some materials more prone to rapid deterioration than others. That said, some of the most obviously fragile man-made materials, including glass and porcelain, are in fact the most resilient.

Collectors react to damaged objects in different ways. Some decide to buy the damaged object in the hope that it can be restored; others shy away from this work and responsibility, preferring to only purchase items in saleable condition. Which type of buyer you prefer to be depends on you, but here are a few points to think about while you make your decision.

• Take the age of the object into account. What is the likelihood of finding another example that has survived in as good or better condition?

ABOVE: Auction houses are great venues through which to buy and sell items for virtually any type of collection.

• Has the price been fairly reduced to take the damage into account?
• *Can* the piece be restored? If so, will this be an easy and inexpensive process?
• If the piece can be restored, will the restoration lower its value?
• Is the object so rare or so essential to your collection that you'd rather have it in its damaged state than not at all?
• Are you going to keep the object and not sell it on? If so, ask yourself if you can live with the damage. If you can, save your money and enjoy the object as is.
• Do you intend to sell the object on? If so, you should know that many dealers and collectors would rather see an object with all its defects and make up his or her own mind on the restoration question.
• Keep in mind that the price of most restored items is about a third of their true value. If the

11

piece is, however, extremely rare to the market – for example, a two-thousand-year-old artefact – most collectors will not be put off by necessary restoration.

• You will probably find that a good many items that you encounter in the marketplace have already been restored at one time or another. Indeed, in the 18th and 19th centuries, personal effects were highly valued, and even crude restoration was a way to keep an item in the family.

• If you do decide to go the restoration route, make sure to check that the restorer you choose is competent and knowledgeable enough to take on the job to hand. In other words, always use a professional. Every type of item has its own specialist, whether it be china, glass, silver, porcelain or furniture.

• Always consider the amount of the restoration cost against the true value of the restored item. If the former is more costly than the latter, you might want to think again.

Spotting a fake

It can be very disheartening to be busily amassing a fantastic collection when all of a sudden you find out that some of your favourite items in it are fakes! This gut-wrenching occurrence is best avoided altogether for obvious reasons. Drawing on my

BELOW: Holmegaard glass is beautiful but delicate. A scratch can result in devaluation.

experience as an antiques dealer and in the salesroom, here are a few tips on spotting fakes that I've picked up along the way.

• Find out as much about the item as possible (see 'Do your research', pages 9-10).

• Study the item in question and look for obvious signs of ageing meant to fool the buyer into thinking the piece is older than it really is. Check the interior and the base of the item for any deceptive markings. You should also smell the item, as pungent chemicals are sometimes used to age items.

• When buying at auction always read the catalogue description closely. If the description reads 'in the style of' or 'after', then the item is a reproduction.

• Consider the material, craftsmanship and style variations typically associated with the object. Does the object that under consideration look and feel like you think it should?

• If the price is inordinately low, you should be suspicious. Why is it so low? Is it the bargain of the century – or just a fake?

• Generally speaking, if the value of an item is high, or if the item is currently very popular with collectors, there will often be forgers out there trying to copy originals to sell on to unsuspecting buyers. So beware of a marketplace suddenly flooded with a particular item.

• It may be worthwhile visiting a shop that actually sells reproductions of the item you collect in order to familiarise yourself with what a reproduction actually looks like. You could also try engaging the salesperson in the hope that you may pick up a few tips on the differences between the reproduction and the real thing.

• Always be sure to get a receipt from any seller. Authentic sellers ought to provide written documentation that states the age of the object and the price you have paid for it. If this is not forthcoming, be suspicious.

Rules to collect by

As you know, I have been collecting antiques – both of the 'present' and of the 'future' variety – for many years, and over this time I have learnt some valuable lessons which I would like to impart to you now. Here are my top five pieces of advice for beginning and maintaining virtually any collection.

1. Spend the most you can afford on the best possible example to get the best possible return. Here is a story to illustrate this point. In 1975, my friend, David Dickinson, was asked to procure a Minton Majolica Peacock for a client. Modelled by the sculptor Paul Comolera around 1873, it is believed that there are only eight examples of the Peacock in the world. David found one in Australia and procured it for his client for £8,000. In 2006, the Peacock was valued at £117,000, based on the retail price index. Not a bad return on an investment that was held and enjoyed for 30-odd years!

ABOVE: The streets and markets are full of knock-off Gucci bags, so buyer beware!

2. Sometimes it is worth selling a few pieces from a collection on in order to buy one exceptional example. Many collectors will start out by investing in the more common patterns or designs within their chosen field, but as their knowledge builds, many will want to invest in better, bigger or more rare designs.

For example, my wife Lesley is an avid collector of 19th-century cranberry glass. A few years ago, it was becoming obvious to both of us that her collection was slowly growing out of its show cabinet, but it wasn't until an impressive five-branch cranberry glass epergne was up for auction at £700–£900 that Lesley thought of selling anything from her treasured collection. Within days, 15 early-day purchases from Lesley's collection were entered into my next auction. Each of the pieces up for auction had cost no more than £25. With my help, Lesley raised just over £1000 and became the proud owner of the cranberry glass epergne which has adorned our dining table for a good many years now.

3. Try to avoid following trends in the marketplace, as prices for trendy items are often higher than they merit. Follow your instincts: if you think the craze for a certain object is a passing fad, then it probably is. Spotting the fads and changes in antiques is all about reading and keeping ahead of the game. The *Antiques Trade Gazette* is a great resource for this type of information. Published weekly, it gives the reader auction reports and prices, and helpfully highlights unusual trends.

4. Seek advice from a friendly collector or expert. Asking these people questions will often reap huge rewards. Specialist dealers and collectors possess vast knowledge acquired by experience and time, and most will share their expertise with other buyers or collectors.

5. Keep a detailed catalogue of your purchases, including such information as when and where you bought the item and how much you paid for it. Keeping such a record will help you to monitor the item's increase (or decrease) in value, which is useful for price comparisons in the future. You should also keep a brief history of where you bought the item, how much you paid for it and any history particular to the item, such as that pertaining to its pattern, shape, number and designer. Yet another, albeit rather morbid, reason for keeping such a record is that upon your demise the inheritor of your prized collection will possess a detailed history for valuation purposes!

13

LOT 1: DIGITAL WRIST WATCHES 1970-1980

The chunky, stylish digital watches of the 1970s were the first to take advantage of electronic micro-circuitry technology. When Quartz-driven digital watches arrived on the scene at the beginning of the 1970s, it was the American and Swiss manufacturers who jumped on the bandwagon most successfully.

In 1971, US company Hamilton Watch Company produced the Pulsar, the world's first wrist watch with no moving parts. This was the first LED (light-emitting diode) solid state digital watch to come on the market. A year later, in 1972, Swiss manufacturer Longines released its first LED model. The cost of producing the liquid crystal display (LCD) soon fell, and those made in the Far East soon flooded the markets. By the end of the 1970s, most watchmakers in Switzerland had reverted to making traditional watches.

Many examples of collectable digital watches can still be found at car boot sales, collectors' fairs and even in vintage clothing shops. With the growing market for all things '70s, they are already going up in price.

Items to look out for
• Casio 505 Data Bank LCD wrist watch on a steel bracelet, c.1980s.
• Pulsar Sport Timer LCD wrist watch on an original black plastic strap, c.1970s. Expect to pay £100 for a good example.
• Fairchild Timeband LCD wrist watch with gold-plated bezel and gold-plated bracelet. Although relatively cheap at £50–£80, its price is sure to rise.
• Synchronar 2100 solar-powered divers' watch. Top-of-the-range stainless-steel strap bracelet with LED readout. Designed by Roger Riehi with a unique double solar panel fitting at the top which could power the watch for up to a year, this complex watch will set you back between £1,000 and £1,500.

TOP TIPS
• Check that all of the watch's functions are in good working order, and that there are no battery leakages, which will ruin the movement.
• Replace or remove watch batteries as soon as they run out.
• Always try to buy watches with original papers, labels and packaging. This will enhance their value.

14

LOT 2: ENAMEL PATCH BOXES –
18TH AND 19TH CENTURIES

Enamel patch boxes were first produced in Europe in the early 18th century, and were used as containers for snuff or patches (beauty spots), as well as tokens of love and souvenirs. Early 18th-century enamels were hand painted, but the introduction of transfer printing in the mid-18th century lead to increased production.

Bilston in Staffordshire was one of the main centres for enamelling, and its snuff boxes and small boxes have become very collectable. Many bear inscriptions such as 'The Gift of a Friend' or 'Britannia Rules the Waves'. Birmingham factories were equally prolific, with most boxes painted on a white background, depicting a copy of a painting or a portrait. They often have a wire basket-shaped base. Battersea and Staffordshire enamels are also collectable. The Staffordshire enamel decoration is usually enclosed within a panel of raised white or gilded enamel scrolling.

In the mid-1970s a London-based company called Halcyon Days began producing slightly more affordable enamel boxes.

Items to look out for

• A contemporary enamel box depicting Elvis Presley after Andy Warhol, issued to mark the 25th anniversary of Elvis's death in 1977. Expect to pay £100–£120.
• A contemporary enamel box produced by Halcyon Days to commemorate the fifth anniversary of the death of the Princess of Wales. This will set you back £100–£120.
• An enamel Easter egg, the 29th in an annual series made by Halcyon Days. The first egg, produced in 1973, is very covetable.
• A Bilston oval box. Expect to pay between £300 and £500.
• A Birmingham box. Expect to pay from £1,000 to a whopping £10,000.

TOP TIPS

• Look out for examples that were produced as a limited edition or a special collection, as these will be more valuable.
• Also look out for eighteenth-century enamel boxes depicting sporting events – especially hot air ballooning – which are highly prized by collectors.
• Any chips or cracks to the enamel will negatively affect the value of a box.

LOT 3: CARNIVAL GLASS 1920-1960

If you are looking to build a collection of glass but cannot the afford the likes of Tiffany or Whitefriars, then Carnival glass may be for you.

Carnival glass came to the fore in early 1900s America on the back of the popularity of the very expensive and chic Tiffany glass. Several American factories of the period started to spray mass-produced, press-moulded coloured glass with metallic salts, which produced the iridescent look characteristic of Carnival glass. The most popular (and therefore cheaper) colours are orange, amethyst, green and blue. Rarer colours include amber and red, with red being the rarest of all. Carnival glass was also produced with a tortoiseshell effect.

Small bowls and jugs are easily affordable; large bowls and flat pieces were more difficult to make and so tend to be more valuable, fetching up to £1,000, depending on the colourway. With the market at possibly an all-time-low and a wide selection of glass to choose from, this is the time to start building your own little pension fund.

Items to look out for

• Northwood Carnival glass. Distinguished by its strong colour and iridescence, most pieces have an identifiable pattern. Will likely show a good investment or at least hold their value. Vases and fruit bowls cost £15-£30; larger vases, pairs and centre pieces go for £50-£75.
• Japanese-inspired decoration. Most producers created patterned pieces, and Oriental designs are particularly collectable. Vases and fruit bowls cost £15-£30; larger vases, pairs and centre pieces go for £50-£75.
• Fenton Carnival glass. Pieces are normally unmarked, but later reproductions are marked. Vases and fruit bowls cost £15-£30; larger vases and centrepieces go for £50-£75

TOP TIPS

• Look for strong colours and a shimmering effect on the surface. One of the best ways to see the true colour is to hold it up to the light. Choose carefully, as pieces with a weak colour and poor level of iridescence will not increase much in value.
• Check for flaws in the glass by holding a piece against a strong light, or look through a spyglass.
• Look for items from the golden era of Carnival glass: between 1920 and 1930.

LOT 4: ART DECO GLASSWARE 1930-40

This is one area of glass collecting that has been overlooked by serious collectors. This means that prices are still quite low, and you can afford to be selective. Many items from this period have survived, and it's not unusual to see well-known makes at antique fairs and auctions.

One of the most collectable names, Monart, was made by Moncrieff glassworks of Perth, in Scotland, which produced everything from large bowls and vases to small perfume bottles. The greens, blues and pinks used were typical of the Art Deco period. The pattern known as 'paisley shawl', recognisable by its swirling 'S', is popular with Monart glass collectors worldwide. A more affordable make, also from Scotland, is Vasart Art glass. Also produced in the 1930s and '40s, it is similar in style to Monart.

My overall tip for collecting from this period would have to be Whitefriars glass from the 1930s. The Whitefriars glassworks, known at the time as James Powell & Sons, developed a wide range of designs and styles.

Items to look out for
• Whitefriars Wavy, which has wavy horizontal bands. Expect to pay £150-£250.
• Whitefriars Optic, which has thin blue 'wavy' treads. Expect to pay £200–£300.
• Whitefriars Cloudy, Ribbon Trailed and Streaky designs. Expect to pay £80–£150.
• Whitefriars Geometric. These vases are often overlooked by collectors because of their plain design. Expect to pay £50–£150.
• The price varies for Monart glass; depending on quality and detail, it will cost £150–£1,500.

TOP TIPS
• A piece with its original paper label will be more sought after by collectors.
• Try to collect documented pieces. These can be easily traced through company catalogues. Many collectors' clubs can supply back publications.
• Ensure there are no blemishes on the surface and on the inside of the item.
• If you do find damage, get an expert in to polish it away. Make sure neither the base nor around the rim are polished, however, as this will affect not just the value but also the authenticity of the piece.

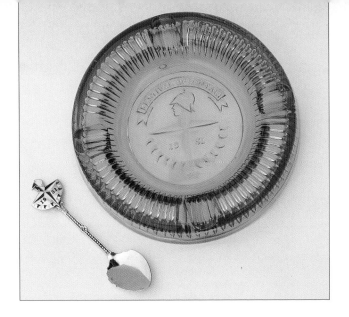

LOT 5: FESTIVAL OF BRITAIN 1951

The Festival of Britain in 1951 was a celebration of the nation's rapid recovery after the Second World War, and a showcase for the arts and sciences and the impact they were having on modern design. Demand for memorabilia from the event is rapidly increasing, as it is for 1950s design in general.

Although the celebrations were nationwide, London's South Bank was the heart of the festival – more than 10 million people came to see The Dome of Discovery, the rocket-shaped Skylon, and other attractions. The Royal Festival Hall, meanwhile, represented the new face of British architecture.

Given that thousands of commemorative objects were produced, many items of Festival of Britain memorabilia can be obtained for under £100, and some for as little as £2! Pieces that were treasured by households at the time are being discarded by subsequent generations, so it's easy to pick up a bargain.

Items to look out for
- Any items by Abram Games, such as the festival logo: a profile of Minerva, the Roman goddess of wisdom and crafts, surmounted on a four-pointed compass.
- Commemorative biscuit tins. These were very popular with collectors in 1951 as they were used again and again. Expect to pay £50–£80 for a piece in good condition.
- Ingersoll pocket watches. The firm produced a range of everyday objects engraved with the festival emblem. These were sold as souvenirs in 1951. A price of around £60–£80 for a working watch would make a sound investment.
- Enamel metal badges. Thousands were produced bearing the official logo, making them easy to find and relatively cheap at £15–£20.
- Ephemera such as programmes for the various festival events. These can be picked up for between £5 and £10.

TOP TIPS
- Go for unusual items from the more notable manufacturers.
- Look out for the superior-quality items carrying the Festival of Britain emblem, as these tend to command a better price.
- Try to collect only those pieces for which the design and colour (light blue or orange) epitomise the period.

18

LOT 6: BOY SCOUT MEMORABILIA

The boy scout movement was founded in 1908 by Robert Stevenson Smyth Baden-Powell, a Boer War veteran, and it soon spread throughout the world. The philosophy of the Baden-Powell movement was expressed in the scout uniform: military-style shorts, a peaked hat, a neck scarf and badges to be earned. All of these items have been collected by enthusiasts for many years. Adding to the charm of this sort of collecting is the fact that many collectors are still involved in the boy scout movement today.

Northamptonshire was the first county to assume a distinctive scouting emblem in 1910, closely followed by Kent in 1912, which used a badge incorporating a white horse. The first badges were made of metal, and these are amongst the most sought after.

During the war years, metal shortages meant that paper had to be used; these badges are also highly collectable. From 1930 the woven cloth badge became universal. Most prized by collectors are badges from counties that are no longer in existence.

Items to look out for

• Badges from 1937–1947 commemorating the Great War Scouting Jamboree. Expect to pay anywhere from £40–£100, depending on condition.

• Any metal badge in good condition. Expect to pay £30–£50 for good-quality badges.

• Hats, scarves (especially pre-1920s), books and photographs. Photographs of King George VI, who was an enthusiastic boy scout supporter, visiting the camps during the late 1930s are particularly prized by collectors of both scout and royalty memorababilia.

• Ogden cigarette cards depicting the boy scouts c.1912. Expect to pay around £40 for a good set.

• Memorabilia from other Baden-Powell groups, such as the Sea Scouts and the Girl Guides.

TOP TIPS

• Condition is extremely important when pricing badges. Any deterioration will have a considerable effect on the price.

• One of the best places to buy and sell such memorabilia is eBay, the online auctioneer.

LOT 7: GARDENING MEMORABILIA

The rapid rise in popularity of garden-related collectables reflects the general public's enduring passion for all things gardening. As the budding market for antique garden pieces gains momentum, certain items will become more valuable. This in turn will lead to mass output of reproduction pieces, which will ultimately affect the market.

A classic example of this pattern has recently been seen with 18th- and 19th-century cast-iron garden urns. A 75-cm (2½-foot) pair of garden urns on stands would have set you back at least £1,000 a few years ago, but with a major influx of reproductions the value has tumbled to £400–£500. Another example of this trend is the current price of original 19th-century Coalbrookdale chairs. Fetching a four-figure sum a few years ago, today a reproduction chair would cost £150–£200.

Items to look out for

• Lawnmowers. Early models have become highly collectable, as are the 19th-century miniature versions made to encourage children into gardening. These are rare but are worth looking out for at £50–£100.

• Cast-iron garden rollers. A favourite amongst collectors, these are still relatively cheap, going for between £15 and £50.

• Watering cans. Look out for 19th-century examples, which would be made from steel. The more unusual the shape, the higher the premium. Copper and brass cans command a higher price than steel ones at £30–£60.

• Terracotta flower pots. These were mass produced in their thousands from the mid-19th century. The addition of the maker's stamp will increase the value, as will an unusual form or size. Art Nouveau-period terracotta pots or wall pots, especially those with a maker's mark, can be found for £100–£200.

• Wooden trugs or baskets. Some examples from the 1920s to 1940s are hard-wearing. Expect to pay between £10 and £30.

TOP TIPS

• More people are using their gardens as additional living areas, and are thus buying all types of garden furniture. These items are therefore in high demand.

• Excessive or poorly done restoration of a garden accessory will have a negative effect on its value.

LOT 8: VICTORIAN FURNITURE 1850-1900

We have all heard it said that Victorian brown furniture has fallen out of bed over the last 10 to 15 years as people have given preference to the modernist look. For this reason, I suggest that now is the time to reinvest in Victorian furniture.

The price of Victorian furniture has been in freefall for the past five years, and has now hit rock bottom. When you can buy a good 120-year-old Victorian chest of two short drawers above three long drawers and with turned handles made by a great craftsman for around £250, you know it is time to snap it up. Rest assured that the Victoriana trend will return.

Items to look out for

• Victorian pedestal writing desks. Made from mahogany, oak and walnut, the desks normally have a twin pedestal to each side containing a flight of drawers above a top section containing three drawers, and with a leather tooled writing area. Try to secure one with the original leather tooling. Expect to pay between £300 and £500.

• Triple wardrobes. These beautifully crafted wardrobes have three sections to the front, and sometimes contain mirrors to the interior doors. Expect to pay between £300 and £750.

• Late 19th-century chiffoniers. A typical chiffonier will have a large mirrored back with shelving above a cluster of drawers and cupboards. Some even contain a wine cellaret. The classic Art-Nouveau-inspired design from the late 19th century will sit well in any modern house. These are grossly undervalued and can be picked up for between £300 and £700.

• Sets of balloon-backed chairs. These extremely comfortable chairs have a circular balloon back, a comfortable, wide seating area and are highly durable. They can be bought in sets of 4, 6, 8, 10 and 12. When considering your purchase it is important to check that each chair is an exact match to the others in the set. For a set of 4 expect to pay £200; a set of 6, £400; a set of 8, £700; a set of 10 or 12, over £1,000.

TOP TIPS

• Try to acquire solid, functional pieces of furniture (they tend to be better quality) in preference to veneered items. Look out for solid oak, mahogany, walnut and birch.

• Check the item of furniture from top to bottom for woodworm! Also, look for alterations, especially to handles and feet.

LOT 9: STORAGE TRUNKS AND CLOTHBOUND TRUNKS – 1900–1940

Storage trunks can be traced back to the 16th century, when they were typically called coffers. From this period you can obtain a lovely oak box with a wonderful patina, and from the 17th and 18th centuries you can get beautiful handmade pieces with dovetail joints and rustic-looking hinges and locks.

Fast forward to the 19th century and you'll find many different shapes and sizes, ranging from a compact 70 x 30cm (27 x 12 in) trunk to a huge 2 x 1.25m (2 x 1½ yd) piece. Some of the more popular examples, like the military-style trunk, have brass inset carrying handles and brass tips to each of the corners. These were normally made from mahogany or oak, with the mahogany examples commanding more of a premium. The top end of the market would be trunks made from camphor wood. This dark, hard wood is highly collectable and gives the interior of the trunk a unique smell reminiscent of aniseed. Even 18th-century examples retain this aroma.

Travelling trunks from the 1900s–1930s, which are solidly made from hessian and bound with strips of oak in a Bentwood style, are very affordable.

Items to look out for
• Seventeenth- and 18th-century trunks. Expect to pay £200–£1,200, depending on size and whether the original hinges and locks are intact.
• Nineteenth-century trunks. Expect to pay £100–£400, depending on the type of wood used.
• Twentieth-century storage trunks were mass produced, so be fussy when making your choice. Expect to pay £20–£70.

TOP TIPS
• Protect the aged beauty of trunks by having a piece of glass made to fit over the top of the wood or cloth. They can then be safely used as coffee tables as they will be protected from spillages.
• When buying a period piece, always check thoroughly for restoration or replacement panels of wood.
• Softer woods from the 18th and 19th centuries are susceptible to woodworm, so check thoroughly for this. If you find signs of woodworm infestation, make sure the item is treated professionally.

LOT 10: BISCUIT TINS

It was not until the end of the 18th century that a technique was developed for printing straight onto metal. The invention of lithographs facilitated this process, which was still, at this time, quite crude .

In 1837 a system was developed in Paris using a chromolithograph (coloured print) which produced beautiful results on metal. By 1860 mass production had started. Benjamin George was one of the earliest manufacturers to design an offset printed technique to directly transfer a design onto metal, and soon after this breakthrough, colourful biscuit tins began to appear, many of which were produced for the Christmas market.

By the end of the 19th century, Huntley & Palmer had emerged as the most prolific producers of printed biscuit tins. They made the design of their tins a speciality, and even produced a catalogue listing their various styles. Many of their tins took the form of everyday objects such as books, ornaments, lorries and cars. These designs are still widely available.

Items to look out for
• Urn-shaped tins made in 1910. Expect to pay £120–£150.
• Huntley & Palmer book-shaped tins from 1901–1910. Expect to pay £50–£100.
• Crawford's Biscuit Bus (the OK3 852). One of these tins sold in 1986, with its original box, for a massive £2,400. Whether this price will ever be achieved again remains to be seen.
• Mass-produced items like the Coronation of 1953 tin or the Queen's Silver Jubilee tin of 1977. These are so plentiful that they will not show a particularly good profit, but they are still must-haves for a biscuit tin collector.
• Any transport-related items. Transport was a fascination for biscuit manufacturers. Look for tins in the shape of lorries, cars, bikes and coaches.

TOP TIPS
• Collecting a theme or specific manufacturer will pay the greatest dividends.
• Try to secure biscuit tins from the 1900s–1930s, as these tins tend to hold their price better than those from other decades.

• As with all fragile items, it is important to check condition. While some wear and tear is acceptable, restoration is not, as it will devalue the item by at least two thirds. Check for signs of overpainting and avoid those pieces.

LOT 11: TRENCH ART 1914-1945

Trench Art is the name given to the souvenirs that serving soldiers during the two world wars turned out in their spare time using fragments they picked up from their surroundings. This art marks a particularly momentous time in history, and offers a fascinating and charming insight into how these soldiers whiled the hours away when they weren't engaged in fighting.

The most common items to be produced were paper knives and ashtrays. These are often crudely made, and typically come with token messages or initials, with the date sometimes scrawled on the bottom of the shell. The dated items have greater collectability.

The most collectable items in this area are, without a doubt, models of ships, planes, tanks or guns. This is the best area of trench art to invest in as not only do these items represent excellent craftsmanship, but they also show great artistic ability. In general, post-1945 trench art is overlooked by many collectors, yet it is a good future investment.

Items to look out for
• Paper knives and ashtrays. Expect to pay £5–£15.

• Lighters. The more expensive versions come with the ashtrays attached. Check the craftsmanship carefully before parting with between £20 and £40.
• Button hooks or desk paperweights. These more unusual items represent a good investment. Expect to pay £20–£30.
• Models of ships, planes and tanks. Although these items are usually unsigned, many can be dated by the shells and materials used. Expect to pay between £60 and £100 for a good example.
• Spent bullet shells. Many of these are currently in use as door stops; I have even seen them used as vases. Spent bullet shells are a fairly common sight at boot sales and antique fairs, where they can be picked up for a few pounds. Jump in quick before the price rises.

TOP TIPS
• You really don't need any specialist knowledge to invest in trench art, just common sense and a tin of brasso.

• Trench art is often undervalued by sellers because of its morbid (in some people's eyes) associations. Capitalize on this sentiment and pick up a bargain.

LOT 12: SUFFRAGETTE MOVEMENT

Important events in history offer the collector an ideal opening for investment. The suffragette movement, founded by Emmeline Pankhurst in the 1880s to peacefully campaign for a woman's entitlement to vote, represents such a opportunity.

After several years of campaigning, a meeting with MPs turned into a confrontation and the suffragettes realized it was time for 'Deeds Not Words'. Many arrests followed for various offences, including assaulting a policeman, protesting in parliament and on the streets, and even chaining themselves to the Prime Minister's front door. Emmeline herself was arrested for common street brawling and sentenced to six weeks in prison.

The battle for the vote continued, with more imprisonments and protests, but at the onset of the First World War the suffragettes suspended all action in order to help defend the country. In 1916 the Government finally acknowledged that women deserved the vote; it had taken nearly 40 years of imprisonment and hunger strikes to get it. Today, items from the suffragette movement are collectable due to this colourful history.

Items to look out for

• Cartoons from the period, which can still be bought from between £10–£50.
• Many postcards were produced around the turn of the century, and these are prized by collectors of both postcards and suffragette memorabilia. Expect to pay around £20–£30 per card, depending on the condition.
• *Punch* magazine produced some suffragette memorabilia in its 1906 January–June edition, volume 130. These items can be bought for £15–£30.
• Among the more collectable items are china, vases and medals. Depending on the size and condition, these items can sell for between £30 and £100.
• Items of jewellery which have direct links to the suffragettes are rare. Expect to pay anything from £200 to £500, depending on the base metal and the decoration.

TOP TIPS

• The suffragette moment presently has a cult following in England, and there is also worldwide interest. Superior returns can be had by selling your items on the Internet.
• Arrive early at boot fairs and antiques fairs, as suffragette items are usually snapped up quickly by the early birds.

LOT 13: VANITY FAIR CARICATURE PRINTS

Vanity Fair was a society magazine published in London from 1869 until 1914 (it is still a leading publication today in the USA). Its clientele was the rich and famous, and its news covered society functions, the royal family and the fashion world.

The *Vanity Fair* caricature prints were always of well-known figures of the day, and were not at all flattering. The cartoons in the magazine were in the form of coloured lithographs, but were sold to the public in coloured print form made from the original plates.

Most of the cartoons are finely executed and measure about 15cm x 30cm (6 in x 12 in), accompanied by a short, witty biography of the subject. The magazines were published in a numbered series, and the most highly regarded examples are those in pristine condition. It is worth remembering that some well-known artists of the day contributed to the magazine, including Phil May and, of course, the famous 'Spy'.

The market value of these prints has fluctuated over the years. With their value now at an approachable price, I think it is time to buy.

Items to look out for

• Sporting prints, especially those featuring cricket and horse racing, are very popular. Expect to pay £35–£75, depending on the subject matter.
• Caricatures of certain politicians, especially ex-prime ministers, are prized. Expect to pay between £40 and £60 for an unframed copy.
• Anything pertaining to the law or the Law Society will hold its price amongst collectors. As many examples still exist, prices are quite low at between £20 and £40 per print.
• Try to collect themed sets. For individual prints, those dating from pre-1900 are the most desirable. Expect to pay £50–£100 for an unframed copy.

TOP TIPS

• Try to steer clear of reproduction prints as these will not represent a good investment.
• Original lithographs from the period will have a plate line on the exterior of the coloured print, and the script and biography must be in place in order for the print to achieve its full value.
• It is essential that the print has no tears or fold marks.

LOT 14: THERMOMETERS

Many weird and wonderful thermometer shapes and designs were produced in the 19th and early 20th centuries, and some highly collectable samples are in existence. Shrewd collectors are snapping up the most unusual examples.

Galileo invented the thermometer in the late 16th century. It was a simple glass tube ending in a bulb; the open end was immersed in water. He noticed that when the water was heated it rose up the tube and could then be calibrated. Over the centuries, it became apparent that this invention could be used to monitor a whole range of everyday events, including the degree of a fever and the weather, as well as for cooking and brewing.

There are many collectable thermometer designs from the 19th and early 20th centuries. Some sport advertising logos; these were often given free to retailers who sold the company's product. Many are suitable for exterior use, while others are decorative and should be reserved for interior use only.

Items to look out for

• Thermometers carrying a company logo. If the company is no longer trading, this will enhance the price. Expect to pay £15–£100, depending on size and material.
• Novelty thermometers from the 1940s to the 1960s can often be found at local boot fairs and charity shops for between £2 and £15. This is an area where a profit can be made.
• Solid brass thermometers from the 19th century. These are still relatively cheap at between £8 and £15.
• Examples with elaborate cases. The more elaborate the casing, the more you should expect to pay. Those with mahogany cases and ivory dials can cost £80–£150. A maker's mark will further increase the price.

TOP TIPS

• Make sure the thermometer is still working. Place your thumb on the bulb at the bottom where the mercury is contained and you should see the temperature rise.
• Always try to keep your thermometer upright when transporting it in order to avoid disturbing the mercury.
• If your purchase was intended for exterior use, do not be afraid to put it in your garden. You'll have a great talking point and it can be brought into the house during the cold winter months for protection.

LOT 15: W. H. GOSS AND CRESTED CHINA

William Henry Goss was the first and arguably the finest-ever manufacturer of crest-ed china. In the 1880s, William's company began to make miniature pieces of china that could be sold cheaply to the ever-increasing number of day-trippers holidaying in popular locations in England. He printed crests and coats of arms of the particu-lar town onto each piece and made different crests for each locality, so that a collector had to travel throughout the entire country to complete his or her set.

W. H. Goss porcelain is easily recognised by its ivory colour and simple crest. It comes in many shapes and styles, including Roman vases, tombs, shoes, clogs, lighthouses and – the most popular of all – replicas of famous buildings and cottages. All items are marked with the Goss back stamp of a goshawk with its wings outstretched.

Items to look out for
It is difficult to collect every piece of Goss porcelain or china, so set yourself a price bracket. I recommend buying the following:

• Yachts or boats. These shapes were difficult to make and were always more expensive when sold new. Expect to pay £60–£80.
• Airplanes and tanks. Highly prized by collec-tors and obtainable for £80–£120.
• Cottages and houses. Look out for Anne Hathaway's or Robert Burns's cottage. St Paul's Cathedral is also a popular collector's item. Expect to pay £40–£80.
• Goss china from 1858–1880 has become increasingly rare. Look for figurines, bread plates and dolls, and expect to pay between £200–£2,000 depending on quality and rarity.

TOP TIPS
• The price of Goss china has fallen over the past ten years. Some dealers don't recognise the rarity of some of their stock and tend to price all pieces the same. This means you can snap up a bargain.
• Make sure there is no restoration or retouching. This can be done quite easily by holding the piece up to the light, as china is translucent.
• Several auction houses sell Goss crested china in job lots, and the value of some of the individual pieces can be as little as £5. If you look hard you could well find a 'sleeper' (a valuable yet unnoticed item) amongst a job lot.

LOT 16: MOUSTACHE CUPS

The moustache cup, a superb invention by Englishman Harvey Adams, is so called because of its unique inner lip, designed to protect the user from being left with a soiled moustache.

First manufactured in 1830, the cups were originally called 'Napoleons' or 'Saucers', presumably because at that time men wore a 'Napoleon' or small moustache inspired by the Franco-Prussian War. They became popular in the USA following the war with Mexico in 1840, when most men in the army and navy had a moustache. By the 1890s their popularity had reached its peak.

A wide range of materials was used in the manufacture of moustache cups, including porcelain, earthenware, tin and silver plate. Most had matching saucers. Initally sold individually, as their popularity grew they were included in tea and dinner services.

Some collectors believe the French-made moustache cups to be preferable, while others prefer those from the German factories, including Miessen and Dresden. Advanced collectors favour cups with Majolica, Imari, Sunderland Lustre, Belleek, Crown Devon or Wedgwood marks.

Items to look out for
• Moustache cups from the 1850s to 1890s will be the most expensive. Expect to pay £40–£100 for a transfer pattern; £250–£2,000 for a fine hand-painted example.
• Late 19th-century examples by well-known factories such as Wedgwood, Worcester and Crown Derby. Expect to pay £50–£120.
• Left-handed moustache cups and saucers.
• Ladies' and gentlemen's sets. Expect to pay £60–£120 for a transfer print.

TOP TIPS
• Make sure that the cup and saucer are a matching pair. Most will have the same back stamp or pattern number. Many American manufacturers had no marks, but the pattern number is still carried on the base of each item.

• Remember that the quality of the painting will determine the price.
• Early 20th-century moustache cup-and-saucer sets are the most affordable. These were normally crested with a town, or with token words. Many were produced in the Staffordshire factories, and are unmarked.

POOLE ATLANTIS

LOT 17: POOLE POTTERY ATLANTIS WARE 1970-1980

Poole pottery has long been a saleroom favourite, and is considered by some to be a blue-chip investment. Pieces from the late 19th century up until the 1980s remain highly collectable, with some investors specialising in a single period from the company's rich and varied history.

Poole pottery, thanks to its design teams, has always been ahead of its time. One of its legendary designers was Guy Sydenham, who joined the company in 1932 and helped create a pattern called Freeform, a minimalist look with hand-painted decoration which was produced from the late 1950s to the early 1960s. Other ranges favoured by collectors are Delphis and Aegean.

Launched in the early 1970s, the Atlantis range was produced in subtle colours such as olive, fawn and brown. Most Atlantis ware consists of vases, but there is also a chess set in the range. As production was concentrated between 1972–1977, output was small. I am tipping the Atlantis range because each item was made and thrown by Guy Sydenham. Many have his signature on the base.

Items to look out for
• The most sought-after pieces are from the early Atlantis studio ware, dating from 1966–1972. These are normally signed and numbered by Guy Sydenham on the base. Expect to pay £200–£400 for small items and up to £1,500 for larger items.
• Highly decorative smaller vases. These will set you back £50–£100.
• Ionian ware. Although little of this ware was produced, it does turn up from time to time normally as highly decorative plates or chargers. Ionian ware is worth keeping an eye out for, as some of the best designers and decorators worked on it during the 1974–5 period Expect to pay between £50 and £100.
• Barbara Linley Adams-designed animal sculptures. Expect to pay £15-£40.

TOP TIP
• The material used for making Atlantis ware was earthenware, which is very fragile and easily damaged. It is thus important to check that there are no chips in a piece, and also that it has not undergone restoration, for both of these factors will lower the value of the piece.

30

LOT 18: EIGHTEENTH-CENTURY SILVER – HESTER BATEMAN 1708-1794

Scholars consider Hester Bateman to be perhaps the greatest ever female silversmith. Her work is particularly popular with American collectors.

Bateman began her career in 1760, making mainly flatware. She favoured spoons, but she soon expanded into a range of domestic silverware, including tea sets, cream jugs, sugar basins and tea caddies. It is thought that her finest pieces are her crest-shaped wine labels and seals.

Many of Hester's descendants went on to become accomplished silversmiths, including her great-grandson, William II.

If you decide to collect Bateman silver, bear in mind that the Bateman hallmark 'HB' was also registered by other silversmiths who had the same initials. However, the date and the shape of the enclosing punch should lead you to a genuine Bateman piece.

Items to look out for

• Single hallmarked teaspoons in good condition. Expect to pay £30–£40.

• A matching set of six teaspoons (be sure to check that the hallmark dates are identical years). Expect to pay £150–£250.

• Medium-sized dessert spoons go for £50–£70, depending on the decoration.

• Sugar tongs (sugar nips) for £60–£120.

• If you fancy spending a bit more, it is worth investing in any of the larger pieces of Hester Bateman silver, which include teapots, cream jugs, sugar basins and wine labels. Most of these items will cost £300–£1,200, but over the years they have proved to be a solid investment.

TOP TIPS

• Beware of forgeries. Hester Bateman silver is thin and tends to be of a lighter weight than that of many of her imitators.

• By acquiring lesser pieces of Bateman silver, such as her teaspoons or sugar tongs, you will learn to recognise the mark, weight and style of decoration, so gaining the confidence to advance your collection onto sugar basins and cream jugs.

• Earlier examples of Bateman spoons will be hallmarked at the base of the shank near the bowl. This marking was replaced in the mid-1770s by the more familiar top marking that sits near the end of the shank.

LOT 19: ART DECO BEDROOM SUITES
1920-1950

The popularity of Art Deco bedroom suites has fallen over the past ten years, possibly because nowadays we tend to live in smaller rooms that are unable to comfortably accommodate these impressive suites.

A complete suite would consist of a double bed, two bedside cabinets, a lady's wardrobe, a gentleman's wardrobe with a dressing chest and stool and a tall boy (chest of drawers). Most suites have been split up over the years, with the pair of bedside cabinets, tall boy and the dressing chest being the most popular with buyers. The larger wardrobes have fallen out of style dramatically.

Much of the beauty of these suites comes from their maple veneer. The more expensive pieces also have maple-lined drawers and interiors. The Art Deco theme is seen most strongly in the handles and fittings; pieces with these intact are popular with collectors.

Items to look out for
• An original bedroom suite from the 1930s with a strong design throughout. Expect to pay £250–£300 at auction.
• Light oak, sometimes called blonde oak, suites are solid and well made. Expect to pay between £200–£500 at auction.
• A 1950s version of an Art Deco suite will cost between £150 and £200 at auction. These suites are not, however, as well made as the 1930s suites.

TOP TIPS
• Buying a complete suite can be cheaper than buying single pieces. The bedside cabinets, tall boy and dressing chest can easily be used in your bedroom, while the wardrobes wait in your garage (storing your vintage clothes of course!) until the time when they are back in fashion. You'll have a complete suite and hopefully a tidy sum.
• Look for dressing chests with a large circular mirror to the back, supported by twin pedestals to the side and united by a shelving unit. You might even find a matching dressing table stool.
• Look for a pattern called bird's eye maple – this is one of the most popular designs from the period.
• Make sure all the Art Deco handles are intact and matching on all the items when buying the complete suite.

LOT 20: TAXIDERMY

Taxidermy involves the removal of the skin, flesh and bones of an animal (with the exception of the skull). The fat is scraped out from the skin and then the remains of the animal is preserved with borax. A wire frame is covered with wadding and the skin loosely arranged and padded with wood wool. Glass eyes are added and the tongue and mouth made of painted plaster. To enhance the realism, animals are given a naturalistic setting, sometimes even with a painted background scene.

Taxidermy came to the fore in Britain in Victorian times; particularly popular were large displays of exotic birds, many of which are in excellent condition today. There was also a fascination for bizarre human-like scenes made from animals, known as tableaux. Walter Potter was perhaps the most famous tableaux maker, with pieces such as The Death and Burial of Cock Robin, The Guinea Pigs' Cricket Match, The Kittens' Tea and Croquet Party and The Kittens' Wedding, which sold for £18,000 in 2003 when Potter's World Famous Museum of Curiosity was closed down and its entire contents sold off.

Items to look out for
• A study of an exotic bird in its original case, painted and with a naturalistic background. Expect to pay £50–£70 in good condition.
• Studies of groups of birds or single mammals, £70–£100.
• Taxidermy studies with a maker's label and accompanying history of the animal, such as where it was shot or caught, by whom and when. Expect to pay £100–£5,000, depending on the quality.
• Tableaux studies. Expect to pay between £800 and £20,000, depending on size, complexity and subject matter.

TOP TIPS
• Look for the following names: Cullingford, Rowland Ward, Spicer of Lemmington, and H. N. Pashley of Cley – specialist taxidermists sought after by collectors.
• Remember that dealers must have a licence to sell specimens.

• Bear in mind that fur, feathers and skin can be damaged by moths and sunlight, making them costly to restore.
• Be wary of reproductions – some have been known to fool even the experts. These are typically fish made from moulded plastic.

LOT 21: RUSKIN POTTERY

Sometimes it's worth investing a large amount in a single antique. In the case of Ruskin pottery, spending £1,000 or more on one item could prove a sound investment.

The Ruskin pottery factory was founded in West Smethwick, near Birmingham, in 1898 by William Howson Taylor and his father, Edward. They took the name for the factory from the famous Victorian writer and critic, John Ruskin.

Most of the items they produced reflected the Taylors' interest in experimental and oriental-inspired glazed effects, with many forms influenced by 18th-century Chinese porcelain, especially the 'flambé' varieties such as 'sang-de-boeuf', 'snake green' and 'peach bloom'. (These are considered among the most collectable.) The majority of Ruskin pottery items are marked on the base with an incise mark of a pair of scissors and the words 'Ruskin pottery' or just 'Ruskin'.

By about 1910, William Howson Taylor had mastered the flambé technique, and was widely recognised as one of the master potters of the modern world. He went on to build on this reputation, and kept his small team of accomplished potters working until 1933, adapting his style over the period to suit the public taste.

Taylor died a couple of years after the pottery closed. Sadly, he had destroyed all of his records, but he did leave us the pottery itself, widely considered to be the work of a genius

Items to look out for
• Lustre ware, especially in lemon, yellow and orange. Expect to pay £200–£700, depending on the size, style and decoration.
• Any piece of pottery inspired by the Orient. Such items will be in the higher price bracket, but they represent a good investment nonetheless.

LOT 22: CARRIAGE CLOCKS

The earliest known carriage clocks were produced in France from 1850, and the crème de la crème are those from 1870–1880, when the decoration and manufacturing techniques had been truly mastered. Many examples from the early 20th century still exist today, and these clocks continue to be manufactured.

Small carriage clocks were usually supplied as part of a dressing set; the larger examples were often used when travelling. French carriage clocks, with their coloured enamel, metal or porcelain dials, are among the most decorative. Some have enamel decoration throughout; these are prized by collectors. The top of the clock has a carrying handle with a small glass eye so that the escapement can be seen. The movement in most carriage clocks is spring-driven, with the French and English models having the best movement.

Carriage clock cases, dials, movements and escapements were all assembled in a special factory. The name on a dial is normally not that of the maker but rather the retailer.

Items to look out for

- Mid-19th-century French carriage clocks with enamel decoration. Expect to pay between £1,000 and £2,000.
- English carriage clocks from the 19th century with a repeater action. Look to pay £400–£600, or £500–£800 if the original carrying case is included.
- Late 19th-century and very early 20th-century clocks with their original cases tend to be overlooked by collectors, and so make a good investment. Expect to pay £60–£150 for a good example without its case; £120–£200 with its original case.
- American carriage clocks are often overlooked, and can be had for £40–£80.

TOP TIPS

- Beware of recently introduced reproductions. These are normally elaborate, colourful and based on the enamel-style decoration of the early French carriage clocks.
- As ever, condition is important. Check the bevelled-edged glass around the clock for chips or cracks and do the same for the enamel dial.
- Clocks with their original carrying case will cost on average £100–£150 more than those without a case. These cases are normally made from animal skin and can be easily restored or repolished.

LOT 23: HEAL'S FURNITURE 1900-1950

The furniture business of Heal & Sons was founded at the turn of the 19th century as a mattress and bed manufacturer. By the late 19th century it had become one of the leading London furniture makers, manufacturers and retailers. The fortune of Heal's is due to the inspiration of one man, Sir Ambrose Heal, who turned the store into a flagship for modern British design.

In the late 19th century, Heal's simple pieces gradually weaned people away from reproduction 18th-century designs – a breath of fresh air for those who had felt stifled by the obsession with Victoriania.

Oak was Sir Ambrose's preferred material for his furniture, sometimes inset with ornate panels. As the 20th century progressed, Sir Ambrose spotted the impending popularity of the Art Deco movement, and Heal's became associated with subtle Art Deco pieces, more accurately described as a cross between Arts & Crafts and Art Deco. By the 1940s Heal's was retailing the work of some of the period's most avant-garde designers, including Lucy Rie, Pilkingtons, Keith Murray, Roger Nicholson and Lucienne Day.

Items to look out for

• A signed edition furniture series designed by Ambrose Heal and released to the public in the early 1930s. Expect to pay anything between £3,000 and £6,000 at auction.
• Sir Ambrose Heal designs from the late 19th-century to the 1920s with a strong Arts & Crafts influence. Most will have retained their original maker's label, which is often inset. Expect to pay around £150 for a small side table; £2,000–£3,000 for larger pieces.
• Furniture from the 1940s to the '60s. A trestle table and six chairs costs £1,200–£1,400.
• Limed or blonde oak furniture from the 1920s–1940s, especially those designed by Sir Ambrose Heal. Be prepared to part with up to £5,000 for signed edition pieces.

TOP TIPS
• Limed or blonde oak furniture, either retailed or manufactured by Heal & Sons from the period 1940 to 1950, is the bargain area for the investor; many collectors have a preference for the early designs.
• Brand labels often fall off pieces of furniture, so check obscure places on the piece (under drawer carcasses, for example) for a maker's stamp, which will usually be there.

LOT 24: SILVER VINAIGRETTES – 18TH AND 19TH CENTURIES

A vinaigrette is a small box that opens to reveal a hinged pierced grille, beneath which lies a fine sponge which would have been soaked in an aromatic substance. Back in the days of the great unwashed, a person might, upon finding the smell of their surroundings intolerable, open their vinaigrette and attempt to obscure the offensive odour.

The golden period for vinaigrettes was from the late 18th century to the mid-19th century. After that time sanitation and personal hygiene improved, rendering them obsolete.

The toy manufacturers of Birmingham's silversmith trade were in the forefront of vinaigrette manufacture. Most of these vinaigrettes have a gilt interior and grille; on earlier versions the grilles have geometric piercings. Later examples are often engraved with leaf patterns. Valuable pieces will feature birds, musical instruments or military trophies. Engravings of well-known castles add value.

Items to look out for
• Birmingham hallmarked silver vinaigrettes in original condition from 1850–1900. Expect to pay £30–£80.
• Pre-1850s hallmarked vinaigrettes. Expect to pay £80–£150, depending on the condition and decoration to the case and interior.
• London hallmarked vinaigrettes represent a solid investment at £100–£300.
• The most famous name to look out for is Nathaniel Mills. Familiarize yourself with the Mills hallmark and you could bag a bargain. You'll pay between £300 and £500.

TOP TIPS
• Beware of any engraved railway or ballooning scenes to the front of a vinaigrette – these will almost certainly be modern engravings that were added later.
• Be suspicious of any rubs to the hallmark on the interior – wear and tear should not occur here.
• When cleaning silver, especially small items, be careful not to apply too much pressure. Use a silver mitt.
• Most vinaigrettes are rectangular shaped and about 3cm (1 in) long. Seek out unusual shapes with elaborate engravings.
• Ensure the hallmark on the interior of the lid matches any other hallmark on the vinaigrette, including the underside of the grille, as these were often replaced.

LOT 25: PORTRAIT MINIATURES – 18TH AND 19TH CENTURIES

Collecting portrait miniatures will bring out the detective in you, as much of the fun is in researching the sitter. This research will pay off, as most collectors will want to know as many details as possible about the sitter before purchasing an item.

The other factors influencing value is the type of metal the frame is made from and the amount of information available on the artist. Miniatures painted on ivory are the most prized examples.

Although portrait miniatures exist from the 16th century, it wasn't until the 18th century that they became a must-have accessory for the rich and famous. By the late 19th century, the emergence of photography had rendered the miniature less desirable.

Research is essential when attempting to buy portrait miniatures. The quality and condition of the painting are initial considerations. If the portrait is unidentified, it may be possible to identify the sitter by visiting portrait exhibitions or looking at reference books. A knowledge of costume history is also necessary to date a miniature with any degree of certainty. I would advise beginners to confine themselves to modest examples to start with.

Items to look out for
• Genuine 18th-century portrait miniatures. Expect to pay £200 to a monstrous £30,000, depending on the artist and sitter.
• Continental 19th-century miniatures are inferior and can cost £40–£70.

TOP TIPS
• Inspect the miniature with a strong magnifying glass for any signs of restoration and any cracks.
• A false signature is common, especially on pieces by a well-known artist.
• Portrait miniatures by well-known artists often turn up framed in a square ivory frame made from old piano keys. Others turn up in a gilt metal frame with bows of metal ribbon decoration at the top.
• Beware overpainting on prints, especially as these are often found in original 18th-century frames. This is when your magnifying glass will be invaluable. The best place to look for overpainting is where the colours are light, as it is hard to conceal the printed line or stipple shading.

LOT 26: SLAG WARE

Slag ware is a type of glass that is found in a huge variety of colour combinations. It has a unique mottled appearance.

Slag ware comes from the Midlands and the industrial North East of England – Gateshead seems to have been the industry's heart and was home to two of the most prolific glass houses from that period, J. G. Sowerby and George Davidson. The origin of the name remains somewhat mysterious. The most likely explanation is that slag ware is so-called because it was made by adding slag from a local steelworks to the molten glass. Slag glass is usually blue, mauve or white, although purple glass can also be found.

Most of the more unusual designs were patented, and consequently these bear registration marks which can be help you identify and date the item. Up until 1883, these marks took the form of a diamond shape containing the day, month and year of design. On top of all these marks would have been a class number (111 for glassware), and somewhere near the diamond would have been the trade maker's mark. Two of the most common markings were the Sowerby trademark, a peacock's head; and the Davidson trademark, a demi-lion rampant over a crown.

Slag ware is at present readily available and reasonably cheap. Very few, if any, dealers specialise in it. During its heyday so much slag ware was made that it is quite easy to build up a large collection today.

Items to look out for
• With so much slag ware available, you can afford to be fussy. Aim to collect only named pieces and concentrate on pre-1883 items.
• Pieces from the better makers will all have a registration mark and a design mark. The prices can be as little as £25.
• Do not overlook plain slag glass, as this is collectable in its own right. Small pieces can be found for the bargain price of between £15 and £50.

TOP TIPS
• Beware of imitation slag ware hailing from Italy and Scandinavia. Most of this is unmarked and does not have the beauty of the original 19th-century glass.
• Basket weave and diamond-cut patterns are the most popular surface textures, and a must-have for any serious collector.

LOT 27: BAMBOO FURNITURE 1900-1930

In the early 1800s the Prince of Wales, later George IV, bought bamboo furniture direct from Canton to add authenticity to his Chinese interiors of the Great Brighton Pavilion. Bamboo was soon to be found in all the great houses of England. It was imported throughout the 19th century, but the popularity of Chinese bamboo was short-lived and the majority of pieces can be attributed to the early part of the 19th century.

Chinese bamboo is hard to date as the traditional methods of construction are still being used today. Look for tightly packed lattice work, a lacquer or cane work surface, banding and stretchers which continue around the outside of the uprights and wooden pegs holding all the joints. If you understand the construction of the piece, you should be able to distinguish early 19th-century examples from 20th-century ones, and so grab a bargain.

At least 90 percent of the bamboo furniture available in the UK is of English origin. During the period 1800–1930 there were over 100 registered producers, many from London's East End but also from Birmingham and Nottingham. A passion for Japanese art in the 1860s fuelled this growth, and lacquered panels, rolls of matting and bamboo poles were imported from Japan in their thousands. These were then made up into jardinières, bedroom suites, pen holders, standard lamps, bookcases and side tables. By the late 19th century one producer claimed to be shipping 4,000 pieces a week all over the world.

Items to look out for
• A two-tier, well-constructed bamboo side table. Expect to pay £20–£50.
• Bamboo chairs can be found for £25–£60.
• More unusual items, such as shelving and bookcases. Expect to pay £50–£100, depending on size.
• Chiffoniers or revolving bookcases for £300–£800.

TOP TIPS
• Bamboo is more difficult and expensive to repair than it looks, so if the item is wobbly, don't be tempted by a lower price.
• Any damage to the lacquer will lower the price. Similarly, avoid any item that has been touched up with paint.
• Many items still have a maker's mark or label intact. These will be more desirable to a collector.

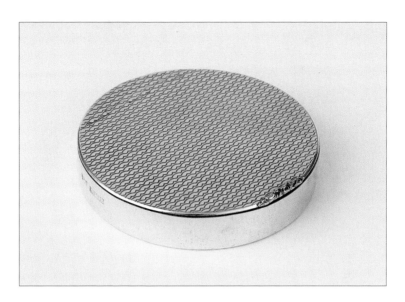

LOT 28: POWDER COMPACTS 1920–1970

Portable grooming kits for women were an essential item after the Second World War, when it became more socially acceptable to reapply make-up in public. The first powder compacts appeared in the early 20th century, mostly imported from France and the USA. By the 1930s the British had started to produce their own compacts. Many were made from sterling silver, but silver plate, chrome plate and gold plate were also used, as well as tortoiseshell, mesh and the very collectable Bakelite.

Compacts came in all shapes and sizes, often bejewelled and sometimes with a mechanism to play music when opened. Some even had a cigarette case and lighter attached!

During the Art Deco period powder compacts had highly sophisticated designs, but this slowly gave way to souvenir designs and novelty items, which are found in abundance in the market today, and which are, consequently, the least sought after. By the 1960s, with the beginning of compressed powder and disposable containers, powder compacts became consigned to history. Yet their beauty and the nostalgia they bring to mind gives them an enduring appeal to the fashion-conscious collector. Today there are many compacts on the market at 'come-and-buy-me' prices, and they make wonderful presents for collectors and non-collectors alike.

Items to look out for
• A mother-of-pearl compact in mint condition c.1940–50s. Expect to pay £60–£100.
• Novelty compacts from the 1950s and '60s. Expect to pay between £30 and £70, depending on the decoration.
• Compacts created by top-end silversmiths such as Georg Jensen can go for up to £600.

TOP TIPS
• Look out for the following makes: Evans, Schick Manufacturing Company, Thorens, Coty-Stratton.
• Any compact with its original carrying case will be more desirable to a collector.
• Never wash any part of a compact, including the powder sifter or puffer.
• Always make sure the hinge is in good condition and that it opens and closes easily. Any defect here will affect the price dramatically.
• Use an old toothbrush to clean powder traces from a compact.

LOT 29: VINTAGE LUGGAGE

In the 1920s and '30s, ownership of a set of custom-made luggage was something only the wealthy could aspire to.

The luggage was made from wooden boxes and covered in fine leather cowhides. In addition to clothes, the trunks would house a minimum of eight pairs of shoes in individual boxes. Women would have a separate piece of make-up or toiletries luggage.

During the Second World War, most manufacturers moved away from the high expense of leather, and the entire market changed when Samsonite discovered they could use canvas for luggage, and completely took over the competition.

The idea of 'keeping luggage' changed with women's liberation. Although many women in the 1950s and '60s were still carrying their mothers' and grandmothers' match-

ing luggage sets, by now luggage had more to do with convenience than status. The world began to see fewer hardwood leather cowhide items and more bargain-price cardboard.

Items to look out for

• Top-quality manufacturers such as Louis Vuitton, Gucci and other Bond Street names will cost a fortune (between £800 and £5,000), so seek out items at boot fairs and garage sales, where tatty leather suitcases which can be cleaned easily cost between £15 and £100.
• Vintage leather briefcases and attaché cases can be bought cheaply if you hunt around. Many of these items will clean up nicely and can be bought for £25–£80.

TOP TIPS

• Stains or smells can usually be tackled by giving your luggage a good rub down and airing in the sun for a day or two.
• Treat leather with cream leather cleaner from any shoe repair shop and apply with a soft cloth. For suede, brush gently with a suede brush to remove dirt. If the dirt seems to be embedded in the leather,

consult a professional dry cleaner.
• Always follow up leather cleaning with a leather conditioner to replace the item's natural oils.
• The hinges on leather suitcases tend to rust. A quick splash of WD40 cleaner will sort this out. Check for perishing on the hinges as this is one area in which repairs are costly.

LOT 30: CLARICE CLIFF: THE 'MAGIC' STILL WORKS!

Some antiques have a gentle look that could kiss you on the cheek while others are so bold they slap you in the face. Clarice Cliff does both. Her unique designs and style truly typify the Art Deco period. The startling contrast between design classics such as 'Crocus' and 'Lugano' and shapes like her 'Yo Yo' vase is extraordinary. How could one person have produced such a variety of designs?

Clarice Cliff brought colour into the lives of ordinary people; she is the people's designer par excellence. Her work attracted a mass market in the 1930s, and it still does today.

Clarice launched her famous 'Bizarre' range in 1928, and by 1930 she was Design Director of a pottery producing only her work. Her most collectable wares were produced between 1928 and '36 – the 'Bizarre', 'Fantasque' and 'Appliqué' ranges. Her work became collectable through the 1960s and '70s. The 1980s and '90s produced some outstanding prices and the market remains buoyant today.

Her centenary year was 1999, celebrated with an exhibition at the Wedgwood Museum in her home town of Stoke-on-Trent. It was visited by over 100,000 people, including her original painters, by then all in their eighties.

Items to look out for
• Minor pieces of 'Crocus' start at £30 but, depending on the pattern or design, you can pay up to £20,000.
• Elaborate patterns, like geometric designs, are prized. Expect to pay £700 and up.
• Landscape scenes are desirable, as are Art Deco designs. These will cost £200 and up.

TOP TIPS
• Some patterns, like 'Crocus', are rare today and are prized by collectors.
• The more classically Art Deco the shape, the more valuable the piece. 'Bonjour' and 'Stamford' are good shapes to look for.
• Some collectors specialise in one or two patterns; others in plates, vases or jugs.
• Damaged pieces should only be restored by an expert. Amateur restoration will further devalue the item.
• Don't be tempted by restored pieces unless the item is rare and you may not get another chance to buy it.

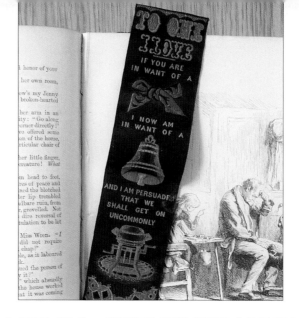

LOT 31: STEVENGRAPHS

A Stevengraph is a small silk woven picture with elaborate patterning, fine detail and strong colours. Most measure 15cm x 5cm (6 in x 2 in).

The first Stevengraphs, produced by Thomas Stevens of Coventry, were launched in great style at the York Exhibition in 1879. The two pictures taken to the Exhibition proved incredibly popular: the first was called 'London and York', and depicted a well-laden stagecoach drawn by a team of four horses; on the mount were the words 'From the Black Swan Holborn London to the Black Swan Coney Street York'. The second picture was called 'Stevenson's Triumphs, 60 miles an hour' and showed the train Lord Howe pulling two carriages. The first examples of both pictures have the 'York Exhibition 1879' monogram.

A stream of silk pictures soon hit the market, depicting famous buildings, sporting and historical scenes and portraits. Stevens also produced silk bookmarks, which were slightly more affordable.

The grandest and largest ribbon of all by Thomas Stevenson was the Great Sash for the Ancient Order of Foresters. The design was registered in 1873, and measured 213cm x 152mm (7 ft x 6¼ in).

The market for Stevengraphs has subsided over the last 15 years, and prices are very approachable. Because Stevengraphs are widely available I suggest targeting certain subjects, such as sporting scenes.

Items to look out for
• Portraits. Expect to pay £10–£40.
• Landscape views in original frames and in good condition. Expect to pay £30–£60.
• Cricket and horse racing scenes for £60–£80; bullfighting, rugby and Victorian cycle races for £100–£150; most other sports for £60–£120.

TOP TIPS
• Look for clean, undamaged pictures with strong colour.
• A remounted Stevengraph will be less expensive, unless it is a very rare example.
• Never reframe a Stevengraph; keep it in its original Oxford gilt frame if possible.
• Keep all coloured silk pictures out of direct sunlight.
• If you intend to collect the Stevengraph bookmarks, make sure the tassels, if any, are intact.

LOT 32: PAPERWEIGHTS 1950-1990

Paperweights originated in Venice in the early 19th century, and quickly became popular throughout Europe. But it was the French who first saw paperweights as beautiful, tactile objects, and it is the French factories of St Louis, Baccarat and Clichy that remain significant for the collector.

Paperweights typically have a thick, clear, domed glass casing which magnifies the colourful design held within. One of the most popular designs contains multicoloured glass canes cut in short sections to create the effect known as *millefiori* (Italian for 'a thousand flowers'). Also popular with collectors are sulphide paperweights, which have a small portrait enclosed in the centre.

The Americans were passionate paperweight producers and their heyday was between 1850 and 1880. Fruit, flowers and animals were the favourite subjects, with a great range of unusual shapes.

Items to look out for
• Weights from 19th-century French factories like St Louis or Baccarat, and good American examples. Expect to pay £400–£600.

• Lalique paperweights. Expect to pay £150–£400, depending on size, shape and design. (The 'R' from the famous signature 'R Lalique' was dropped after his death in 1945).
• Whitefriars paperweights, including *millefiori* examples. These are less common and more valuable than the company's abstract designs from the 1970s. Expect to pay £200–£400.
• Chinese paperweights from the 19th- and early 20th-century are currently underpriced. High-quality clear pieces represent a good long-term investment.
• Pieces by Paul Ysart. A Spanish-born glassmaker who worked for Moncrieff glassworks, his earlier works can be found for under £100. Most have an animal subject to the centre surrounded by *millefiori* design.
• Weights from Wedgwood, John Deakins and Selkirk. Expect to pay around £20.

TOP TIPS
• Always check the interior of the paperweight as the canes sometimes have a maker's mark and date on them.
• Avoid cracked or damaged paperweights – they cannot be repaired.
• Look for closely packed canes and for canes bearing small animal silhouettes.

LOT 33: TROIKA POTTERY

Prices for Troika pottery are high in today's marketplace – they can reach near four figures on some of the larger pieces – but it seems that prices have peaked and are starting to tumble, so now is the time to start buying up this lovely art pottery.

Troika pottery was founded in St Ives, Cornwall, in 1963, by founders Benny Sirota, Leslie Illsley and Jan Thomson. The vision behind the company was to produce pottery as art, with function only a secondary consideration. After a shaky start, the pottery quickly developed a following and a year later, works were being sold in some of the top London stores, including Liberty, Harrods and Heal's department stores.

Following a move to Newlyn in 1970, the factory, although still very successful, closed its doors in 1983. Ten years later, in 1993, the company held a major exhibition of its pottery, and interest was sparked once again.

Troika had two main ranges of ceramics: the smooth-glazed range and the rough textured range. The shapes and styles of the pieces were similar between some of the ranges, but each had its own unique charac-

ter. Today, the rough glazed wares are more popular and are more widely available. The smooth-glazed wares are more rare and are thus more sought after by collectors.

Items to look out for

• Smaller Troika pieces like the preserve and jam pots. These can still be had for £50–£80.
• The tapering coffin vase from the early 1960s. This will cost around £100–£180.
• Lamp bases. These are a bit more pricey and will cost £350–£400.
• The Anvil vase, which will set you back £500–£700.
• Smaller pieces dating from the early 1960s, in particular wheel-shaped vases, which can be had for £75–£100.
• Troika items marked 'Cornwall' on their base were made in the 1970s and will be cheaper than earlier examples, at £40–£80.

TOP TIP
• Many books have been written about the Troika factory, which makes buying Troika easier for the collector, as it is usually possible to date a piece and ascertain its designer. Most books will also give you a chronological history of the markings or back stamps used by the Troika factory.

LOT 34: WEST GERMAN CERAMICS 1950-1970

Do you want to invest in the next 'big thing' in the ceramics category? Then look no further than West German ceramics from the 1950s, '60s and '70s.

These ceramics – mainly jugs and vases – are instantly recognizable with their bold colours and unusual shapes. Many have a volcanic look, with dripping, vibrant colours and swirling or spider's web patterns. Also worth a look are the plain monochrome vases; these are usually embossed with geometric designs.

There were many West German manufacturers producing ceramics from 1950–1970. Many of these items can still be bought for under £20, but that will not be the case for long, so get in quick.

Items to look out for
• Pieces by Bay, Steuler, Ruscha, Jopeko or Sgrafo to maximize your selling-on price.
• Larger pieces such as vases or centerpieces that are decorated with a range of bright colours. The maker is not so important, so long as the piece is marked 'made in Germany' or 'made in West Germany'. Expect to pay £25–£60 for such items.
• Smaller vases, jugs or fruit bowls. These are currently abundant, so you can afford to be fussy with your choice. Try and stick to bright colours, as these are generally the most vaulable. Samples can be had for £15–£35.
• Look for unusual shapes and patterns. These can be worth up to £150, depending on their rarity.

TOP TIPS
• Go for the most brightly coloured vases and jugs.
• Look closely at the decoration, as the quality will vary.
• Always check for hairline cracks. This can be done with a flick of the thumb; if the pot sounds 'dead', then chances are it has a crack somewhere.
• Look for firing fractures in all large pieces of west German pottery. These were mass produced, and many suffered from sub-standard craftsmanship and inspection prior to leaving the factory. Weak points include handles and feet.
• Good places to find these ceramics include boot fairs, antique shops, local charity shops and eBay.

LOT 35: TUNBRIDGE WARE 1900-1930

This is the name given to an exclusively English form of wood mosaic which was first made by local craftsmen in and around Tunbridge Wells, in Kent.

Tunbridge Wells became a fashionable town in which to take one's holiday in the early 17th century, after hot springs were discovered there in 1606. Local craftsmen saw that they could profit from this influx of visitors, and Tunbridge ware was soon being produced in a range of woods and colours.

To make Tunbridge ware, the craftsmen took thin strips of wood of different colours and grains, glued them together and pressed them down tightly in blocks. When the glue was dry, the blocks were cut across in strips. This produced thin sheets of patterned wood which were then applied as veneer to a vast range of objects, including work boxes, candlesticks, writing boxes, jewel boxes, barometers, trays and tea caddies.

As the decades went by, the Tunbridge craftsmen branched out to use a wider range of woods and colourings, so that by the 19th century Tunbridge ware had become one of the best-known forms of wood decoration. By the late Victorian times, pieces were being turned out on a considerable scale.

Items to look out for

Prices for Tunbridge ware are difficult to ascertain, as they really depend on the size, age and quality of the piece. The following list can, however, be used as a rough guide.

• Small stamp boxes and other small Tunbridge ware items generally cost £40–£60.

• Glove boxes and pen holders can usually be had for £80–£100.

• Jewellery boxes, watch stands and small novelty items will cost £200–£300.

• Book slides, writing boxes and visiting card cases can be picked up for £300–£500.

• Pieces attributed to artists Robert Russell or Thomas Barton can cost up to £2,000.

TOP TIPS

• Try to secure items from 1900–1930 as these are inexpensive now, but are sure to rise in price soon.

• Bear in mind that your collection will need a show area in order to keep the items in the best condition for selling on. This can be a glazed book cabinet or a special show cabinet.

LOT 36: PAPIER MÂCHÉ

Papier mâché is made from paper mashed up with water and other stiffeners to make a thick paste, which is then pressed and moulded into various shapes. It is a lightweight material that can easily be decorated with lacquer and paint.

The technique was introduced to France from the Far East from the 17th century, and used in England from 1750. By 1840 papier mâché was at the height of fashion. Many of the items from this period were decorated by highly skilled designer's artists and gilders, and were superbly executed. The quality of work of the Birmingham and Wolverhampton factories in particular was unrivalled.

Trays were the first popular papier mâché items, often with very fine decoration. Soon a range of items was being produced, including boxes, tea caddies, desk accessories, chairs, tables, cabinets, work tables and even beds. These were fragile items, and so collectors took great care of them and they remain in good condition today.

By 1860 the trade was in decline. Some of the major factories were swamped with orders from the Continent, and this lead to a fall in the standard of workmanship, with many items of furniture made which were totally unsuited to the material used.

Items to look out for
• Top-end pieces by Jennens & Bettridge and Ryton & Walton. Expect to pay £300–£1,200, depending on size and style.
• Mid-range small boxes, desk items and magazine racks from the period 1840-1860 can still be secured for £200–£400.
• Papier mâché parlour chairs go for £100–£200; work boxes, snap-top tables and bed ends can be had for £200–£600.

TOP TIPS
• As papier mâché is so delicate, restoration is common. Look out for items having been painted black to disguise restoration.
• On furniture look for weak points like backs of legs and the seating area.
• Check for signs of retouching on the painted and gilded areas.
• Check the quality of the workmanship – after the 1860s the work declined and scruffy examples do exist.
• Some papier mâché items have a still-life of flowers to the centre. This will greatly enhance the value.

LOT 37: BRITISH MARINE PAINTINGS C. 1900-1940

Choosing a painting theme to collect is purely down to individual taste. There is one theme, however, that many collectors are passionate about: marine paintings.

In 1673 the van de Veldes, the father and son Dutch marine artists, laid the foundations for the practice of marine painting in England. Their works, along with countless others produced during the 19th and 20th centuries, ultimately led to a standard type of portraiture: the accurate depiction of a ship (the sea and sky were secondary considerations). Other marine painting subjects included trawlers at sea, as well as coastal, beach, harbour and port scenes.

Oil and watercolour paintings of marine scenes represent a good investment, especially those by known artists. Some hidden talents also appeared from the 1890s to the 1950s; works by these lesser known artists will likely gain in value over the next decade.

Here are some artists worth buying if you get the opportunity: William Charles Cluett (1868-1958), George Hamilton Constantine (1875-1967), Fredrick Dade (1874-1908), R.H. Neville Cumming (1890-1911), Gordon Ellies (1920-1978), Wilton Lockwood (1861-1914), Lewis Mortimer c.1920's-1930's, Aubrey Ramus (1895-1950), Thomas Sydney Moran (1837-1926), and F.P. Taylor (1905-1920).

Items to look out for

• Victorian marine pictures by unknown artists; these will generally go for £100–£200.
• Edwardian and Art Deco period unknown artists; these are a bargain at £50–£100
• Paintings from 1940–1960 are still good value; many cost less than £50.

TOP TIPS

• As with all art perspective, quality and talent should be paramount in your consideration regarding whether to purchase and what price to pay.
• Check for fading; watercolours will fade if kept in direct sunlight.

• Foxing is a minor problem, but a restoration expert will need to be called in.
• An original frame will enhance the charm and price of a piece.
• If you know the location of the subject of the painting, try to sell it in that location, as it will likely fetch the highest price there.

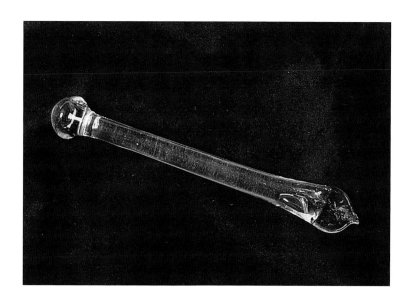

LOT 38: SUGAR CRUSHERS – 19TH CENTURY

Sugar crushers make wonderfully funky cocktail stirrers, so why not get in now and invest in something that will not only impress your friends, but will also make you a tidy profit!

Tracing the history of the sugar crusher is far from simple. It is believed that it was invented in the 18th century, when it was impossible to buy bags of granulated sugar – one had to break a lump off a sugar loaf and place it in a drink using sugar tongs. The sugar crusher was then needed to grind the softening lumps against the inside of the cup or glass.

The prime time for the sugar crusher was definitely the mid-Victorian period. Most were made in glass, and ranged from clear rods with simple, flattened ends to more intricate crushers with elaborate ends squeezed between patterned moulds. The most ornate examples are twisted like barley sugar, and measure between 12cm–17cm (5 in–6 in)

long. The Victorian sugar crushers are rarely recognised as such, as many people mistake them for cocktail stirrers. It is thus possible to buy a sugar crusher for as little as 50 pence.

Items to look out for
• Top-end, solid silver 18th-century crushers for £150–£250. Good luck finding them though, as these are extremely rare.
• Candy-twist, coloured glass sugar crushers. Expect to pay between £25 and £50 if the retailer knows what he is selling. If the seller thinks they are cocktail stirrers, you may need to part with no more than £5–£10.
• Clear-glass 19th-century or early-20th-century sugar crushers for 50 pence to £5.

TOP TIPS
• Silver sugar crushers are extremely rare and they can be quite costly. Easier to find are examples in Sheffield silver plate from the late 18th century, which can still be secured inexpensively, typically for the bargain price of £15-£20.

• Most good silversmiths can re-plate a sugar crusher with little difficulty. Furthermore, because it is a small item, the cost is inexpensive. Best of all, professional re-plating is acceptable to most collectors.

LOT 39: SUNGLASSES 1950s–1980s

Sunglasses first appeared around 1880, but they only really became fashionable when Hollywood stars like Joan Crawford, Cary Grant, Humphrey Bogart and Charlie Chaplin were photographed wearing this trendy new eyewear.

One of the first sunglass manufacturers, Rayban was founded in 1937. During the Second World War, Rayban developed the G15 lens to improve the performance of fighter pilots, and this is when their iconic design, the 'Aviator' model, shot to popularity. Throughout the 1950s and '60s, Raybans epitomized style and rebelliousness. A Hollywood link emerged, with Raybans worn by Marlon Brando in *The Wild One*, Peter Fonda in *Easy Rider* and, more recently, Tom Cruise in *Top Gun*.

Wraparound sunglasses were popularized by the jazz musicians of the 1950s. Also produced during this decade was a range of novelty shades with decorated plastic frames, which are also highly collectable. With the 1960s came the wire-framed 'John Lennon' glasses, and the 1980s saw the return of the

Rayban Aviator and Wayfarer models, now with a 'retro' twist.

Items to look out for

Whichever decade you choose to collect, it must be right in terms of both style and colour.
• Women's novelty sunglasses from the 1950s and early '60s, with outrageous frames and sometimes floral or pierced wraparound decoration. Expect to pay £50–£60.
• Raybans from the 1950s and '60s. Try to source unusual shapes, but beware of fakes. Expect to pay £70–£120.
• Fostergrant's 1970s sunglasses. Seek out unusual shapes and designs. Expect to pay £20–£50.
• Bow-tie-shaped sunglasses. Original examples from the 1940s, '50s and '60s can go for £15–£100, depending on the manufacturer.

TOP TIPS
• Beware of scratched lenses or damaged frames; these will obviously reduce the item's value.
• Fakes are common. If possible, check against a pair you know to be genuine.
• To spot fake Raybans, hold the lens up to the light and you should see a small monogram 'BL' in the corner. If you don't, the glasses are fake.

LOT 40: EARLY PHOTOGRAPHIC POSTCARDS 1890-1940

The world's first picture postcards appeared during the last years of the 19th century. As photographic techniques progressed over the following decades, more people took up photography, often just as a hobby. In fact, some of the rarest photographic postcards were taken by amateurs.

Photographic postcards can be seen as direct descendants of cabinet portrait photographs, or 'cartes de visite'. These were produced in their millions in the second half of the 19th century, but with the introduction of the dry plate process in the early 1870s and of celluloid film in the late 1880s, together with the appearance of more advanced cameras with shutter mechanisms, the taking and making of photographs conforming to the postcard format was easy for most developers.

Most early photographic postcards were topographical, and the majority were turned out by well-known firms, among them Fred Judge of Hastings, Wilson of Aberdeen and Thrift & Co of Reigate. While these are high in quality, they are not the most collectable, as it is actually the subject matter of the postcard that determines its collectability. The name of the photographer is equally unimportant.

By the early 20th century the picture postcard was having its heyday, with photographs of processions, weddings, transport and shops among the most popular. Building a collection from the period 1890–1940 would represent a good investment.

Items to look out for
• Top-end late 19th- and early 20th-century postcards depicting transport, including bicycles, horse-drawn carriages and aeroplanes. Expect to pay £30–£70.
• Documentary postcards, family portraits and shop fronts. Expect to pay £5–£20.
• Panoramic landscape scenes. Expect to pay £5–£20.

TOP TIPS
• Condition is important, but some fading and foxing is acceptable. Remember that these early photographic postcards are actually real photographs.
• Concentrating on one particular subject-matter will probably bring the greatest financial reward.

LOT 41: BAKELITE

The market for Bakelite has been going from strength to strength over the past 25 years, yet there are still opportunities to pick up a bargain.

An unmountable, transparent but easily coloured resin created by the reaction of phenol and formaldehyde with alkaline, Bakelite was first discovered in 1872, but it was its rediscovery in 1907 by L. H. Baekeland that really brought this most durable of early plastics to the fore.

Bakelite is suitable for anything from jewellery to light switches, tea sets to radios. The most popular colours are mottled blue, green, cream and brown. Other forms of Bakelite are made from Vulcanite or Ebonite, both of which are made from rubber. Although all Bakelite is quite brittle, much of it has survived. The opportunities to collect are therefore considerable.

Items to look out for
• Art Deco-period radios from the 1930s. The stronger the Art Deco design, the more desirable the item. The most famous is the Ekco AD75, which can be worth as much as £700–£800. For other models, expect to pay between £150 and £500.
• Dressing table sets. Many were made to simulate ivory or tortoiseshell. A complete set comprising twin candlesticks and jewellery trinket boxes with a ring stand can be worth between £120 and £150. Other dressing table items include manicure sets and vanity mirrors. Beware the cheaper versions.
• Smoking memorabilia, although out of fashion now, was a popular Bakelite item. Look for ashtrays, cigarette holders and cigarette cases of various shapes and designs. Expect to pay £5–£30.
• Bakelite jewellery has become trendy and expensive over the last few years, but an unsuspecting trader might just mistake Bakelite for a cheaper plastic.

TOP TIPS
• Colour variations will make individual items more collectable – a pink mottled vanity set will be worth more than a plain brown one, for example.

• Bakelite is almost impossible to repair, and any damage will be reflected in the price. Hold the item up to a strong light to check for evidence of repairs and for cracks.

LOT 42: TUREENS

The earliest tureens date from the late 18th and early 19th centuries. They were made from porcelain and hand painted, and are a class above the later, run-of-the-mill earthenware tureens.

Most tureens from the late 19th and early 20th centuries were based on earlier styles, and were often designed by top factories, including Wedgwood, Miessen, Vienna and Spode. One of the most popular is the Masons Ironstone tureen, which normally has a Chinese decoration.

There was a time when it was considered highly decadent to serve one's vegetables in a tureen with a lid which matched one's dinner service. But as dinner service items were broken, many tureens were discarded. Unlikely as it may seem, you can buy antique porcelain tureens for £5–£15 in junk shops today – less than the price of contemporary equivalents.

Tureens come in a huge variety of colours, patterns, shapes and sizes. There is no need to be fussy when collecting tureens and lids. A mix-and-match piece is just fine – as long as the lid matches the base!

Items to look out for

• A top-end, 19th-century hand-painted porcelain tureen with a lid and on its original stand will cost between £100 and £500, depending on the factory, size and design.
• Earthenware tureens from Masons, and Ironstone and Staffordshire unmarked tureens and lids. Expect to pay £50–£80.
• Tureens and lids from the Art Deco period right up to the 1970s can currently be found at almost giveaway prices. Go for strong, banded colours and minimalist design. Grossly underpriced at between £5 and £25.

TOP TIPS

• A tureen with its original lid and plate stand will be more valuable.
• Always check that the registration number or design number is marked on the lid, the tureen base and the stand. This will help ensure that you have a matching set.

• Porcelain tureens from top factories like Coalport, Wedgwood and Miessen represent a good investment.
• Check for signs of restoration, as this will affect the item's price. This is quite simple to investigate: hold the item up to the light to reveal any flaws or cracks.

LOT 43: JIGSAW PUZZLES

Jigsaw puzzles can be a very cheap and fun area to collect. They were prolific in the 1900s through to the 1930s, before the advent of television, when they were a great form of entertainment for the whole family.

Jigsaw puzzles were invented by a London cartographer named John Spilsbury in 1760. He mounted a map on a sheet of mahogany, and then cut it out into small pieces with a fine saw so that he could teach his pupils about geography.

The idea caught on, and was copied by other manufacturers. Along with geography, the main jigsaw themes during this early period were religion, history and mythology. Jigsaws dating from this period were all hand-made and quite expensive, but they were popular with the public nonetheless.

It wasn't until the end of the 19th century that a coloured label showing the finished puzzle was pasted on the tops of the jigsaw box lids. At the same time, techniques improved in the making of the puzzles, and mass production began in the early 1900s. By the 1920s, jigsaws had become a craze.

Famous firms who produced these early jigsaws included Chad Valley, which created some incredible jigsaws of the Great Eastern Railway, and shipping lines like the Cunard and White Star lines. Other popular and prolific early producers included Dean & Son, W. Peacock and J. Betts.

Items to look out for

• Puzzles from Chad Valley are very collectable, and for examples from the 1920s and '30s you should expect to pay £40–£60, depending on size and condition.

• Look out for puzzles in which the pieces are shaped like animals. These puzzles were a fad in the early 1900s. Expect to pay £20–£50.

• Advertising puzzles, which were given away free with products like toothpaste and soap in the 1930s. These will cost £30–£60.

• Look out for examples from Par Puzzles, the Rolls Royce of puzzle makers, from the 1930s–50s. Expect to pay £75–£100.

TOP TIP

• Most boxes state how many pieces should be in the puzzle. Although it is obviously difficult to stand and count the pieces if buying a puzzle at a fair or auction, this is time well spent, as they must be complete.

LOT 44: 1950s POTTERY

Pottery from the 1950s really does have a unique design and look. Bouncing back from the depressing war years, many potteries decided to introduce flamboyant, exciting designs, perhaps to cheer people up!

Many potteries from the 1950s have already been widely acknowledged as collectable, and none more so than the 1950s Homemaker pattern, with its distinctive black-and-white designs by Enid Sweeney for the Ridgeways pottery. In its day, the average price for a piece was six pence, but items are now worth on average £10, with coffee pots and teapots worth £50 and upwards.

Collectors should keep their eyes open for Midwinter designs from this period, as Midwinter employed and commissioned many top artists and designers to work on their wares, including Terence Conran. Many of these artists put their names to their designs, and these are often marked on the base.

Items to look out for
• Companies like T. G. Green & Co, well known for their blue-banded ware, went on to produce a range known as 'Blue Domino', with a vivid polka-dot design. Water and cream jugs are now worth £30. Another pattern to look out for is 'Central Park' c.1957; most pieces can be bought at the moment for £10, and they are sure to rise in price.
• Colin Melbourne's designs for Midwinter. His cat figure from 1956 will cost £80–£100. Look out also for his other designs: an animal vase c.1956 for Beswick will go for £60–£80; and the 'Memphis' vase c.1960 for Crown Devon will go for £30–£40.
• The Woods company is one to follow. Their unusually shaped teapots and dinnerware can be bought for under £5. Woods also produced a pattern called 'Pizzaware', a truly inspired shape and pattern c.1950. Vases from this range are still only £10–£15.

TOP TIPS
• Top factories like Rosenthal and Royal Copenhagen employed some influential designers from the 1950s, which are worth seeking out. A bit of research will be likely be needed to accurately date these pieces.
• Designs from Poland and Czechoslovakia make use of a bright palette, and both countries have a distinctive style. Pottery from these countries is worth collecting.

LOT 45: PLASTIC DOLLS 1950s-1980s

Many collectors are aware that the early bisque-headed dolls are worth collecting, but far fewer are aware of the value of plastic dolls. Plastic dolls were mass produced and sold in vast numbers, which means that there is now an investment opportunity for the discerning collector.

Prior to the 1950s, dolls were generally made from bisque and porcelain. But by the 1950s, plastic had become the leading material.

First introduced in 1959 in the USA, Barbie is surely top of the list for the collector. The very first Barbie ever made has been priced at approximately £4,000, and all pre-1970 models are valuable. A Barbie doll can easily be dated to a period by her design. (Note that the dates you'll find on her body indicate a patent date, not the year she was made.)

Another doll to look out for is the Sasha-designed doll. Designed to break down cultural barriers, it had realistic features, with a range of hair, eye and skin colours. Other names to look out for are Pedigree, Terri Lee, Mattel, Mary Hoyer and W. Gobel.

Items to look out for
• Pre-1972 Barbies with original packaging, outfits, hair and clothing. Expect to pay anything between £80 and £400.
• Most of the top doll-makers are well known to collectors, so it's worth sourcing lesser-known makers of plastic-headed dolls. Unmarked and un-named dolls can still be picked up unboxed for £10–£40, boxed for £25–£100.
• Articulated and movable dolls from the 1980s and '90s. One collecting area which is bubbling under is Tiny Tears. This was a doll which accepted water from a bottle and then wet its nappy. Expect to pay £50–£80. Similar versions exist and can be snapped up for £20–£40 boxed.

TOP TIPS
• Ensure the doll's hair has not been cut – it is impossible to replace or repair.
• Ensure the doll represents the period in which it was made by checking the style of the dress, hair and the overall design.

• Keep your eyes open for original dolls' clothing; these items can be valuable. Clothes must be clean and unfaded.
• Any original accessories must be intact.
• The inclusion of the doll's original base, if one existed, will add to the doll's value.

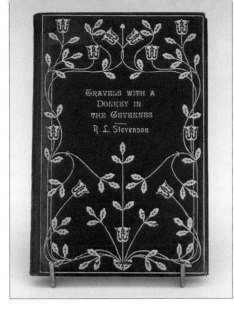

LOT 46: MODERN FIRST-EDITION BOOKS

The author's popularity, coupled with the rarity of the book, will determine the price of any first edition. An author's original appearance in print, whether a first novel or some rather dull poetry, is of particular value if that author went on to greater things.

Noteworthy first novels include *Casino Royale* (1953), by Ian Fleming, now worth between £15,000 and £20,000; *Dead Cert* (1962), by Dick Francis, worth between £1,000 and £2,000; and *Knots and Crosses* (1987), by Ian Rankin, worth between £1,500 and £2,000.

In 1997 Bloomsbury published the first book of a completely unknown writer, J. K. Rowling. She had struggled to find a publisher and only 300 copies of *Harry Potter and the Philosopher's Stone* were issued. Many were given to local libraries and to some lucky schools. Copies now go for over £10,000.

Items to look out for

• Some titles are collectable because they are the author's major work, either by consensus or occasionally because of television or film exposure. For example, prices for first editions of J. R. R. Tolkien's trilogy, *The Lord of the Rings* (1954–55), have soared in the last decade. A fine set might be worth between £18,000 and £25,000 at present. With renewed interest due to the film, this is likely to continue.

• If a title has created a sensation of some kind, collectability will be enhanced. *Lady Chatterley's Lover*, by D. H. Lawrence, was considered unpublishable in England until 1960 because of its graphic sexual descriptions. The first edition, limited to 1,000 signed copies, is now worth between £3,000 and £4,500. Oscar Wilde's prosecution for homosexuality lent particular significance to his *Ballad of Reading Gaol*, which was inspired by his incarceration. The first edition, limited to 800 copies, was published in 1898 and is now worth between £500 and £1,000.

TOP TIPS

• The smallest nick to the spine, or the tiniest patch of rubbing or fading, can affect a book's value enormously.

• If the book had a dust-wrapper, this must be present and in good condition.

• Misprints, one-offs and signed copies are highly collectable.

• Illustrations by a famous artist will make a book more collectable.

LOT 47: BJØRN WIINBLAD CHINA C.1960

The Dane Bjørn Wiinblad was a prolific and multi-talented artist. His output included posters, book illustrations, textiles, glass, porcelain, ceramics and interior design pieces. All of his works are inspired by folk tales, spirits and elves, and his unique style is instantly recognisable.

Most people associate Scandinavia with simplicity and purity in design, but Wiinblad offers something different – something colourful, busy and bold. His studio pieces and one-off examples will be out of most collectors' price brackets, but his china and porcelain is well within reach, particularly the mass-produced pieces he created for the Nymolle and Rosenthal factories.

Wiinblad's early works for the Nymolle factory from around 1960 feature bold portraits and stories, normally in an abstract design. His Nymolle work is easily identified by the body colour in pink, blue, green, brown or black. Most of these pieces can still be picked up for £25–£45.

Items to look out for

• In the late 1960s and early '70s, Wiinblad moved away from mass production back to extravagant hand-crafted pieces with distinct patterns. These will set you back between £350 and £600.

• The 'Flora' range produced for the Rosenthal factory. Many designs are available, with the vase being one of the most popular items in the range to collect. Expect to pay £30–£60.

• Wiinblad's work for the Nymolle factory. A range of small bon-bon or pin dishes was produced in a pattern called 'Praline 1', depicting a woman with extravagantly decorated hair. Expect to pay £15–£30.

TOP TIPS

• Bjørn Wiinblad died in June 2006, and so his pieces are sure to rise in price.

• Always check that the piece is signed. Wiinblad's flamboyant signature is usually found below the manufacturer's mark.

• Always check for damage – a gentle tap should produce a clear sound. If the vase is faulty you will hear a dull thud instead.

• Wiinblad produced a range of Christmas plates for Rosenthal from 1971 to 1982. These are fast becoming collectable.

• It is worth buying duplicate pieces, as they will rise in price for selling on.

LOT 48: SCANDINAVIAN GLASS 1960s-1980s

Glass has been a key area of antique collecting for the past century. The last 'big things' in glass were Whitefriars and Geoffrey Baxter, and I am tipping Scandinavian glass from the 1960s to the '80s as the hot trend to come.

In Scandinavia, glassmaking pieces were blown into moulds, allowing high output and consistency between individual items. Most Scandinavian styles have geometric, angular shapes in jewel-like colours. Nature and the Scandinavian landscape were also important inspirations to glassmakers from the period, with textured surfaces similar to ice and bark. Organic asymmetric forms and optical effects were similarly popular, and can still be found at affordable prices.

Items to look out for

• The companies to look out for are Riihimaen Lasi Oy, Holmegaard Glassworks, Kosta Boda, Orrefors, Kastrup-Holmegaard and Nuutajarvi Notsjo. Noteworthy designers are Nanni Steel, Helena Tynel, Vicke Lindstrand, Tapio Wirkkala, Timo Sarpaneva, Per Lutken, Otto Brauer and Michael Bang.

• Pieces signed by the artist, especially from top factories such as Costa and Orrefors. Some factories signed their pieces with initials and dates; others carry the full signature. Signed pieces by Vicke Lindstrand for Kosta Boda are sometimes initialled 'LH'. Expect to pay between £100 and £300, depending on the design, style and size.

• Look for pieces with a minimalist look that resemble 1960s and '70s Whitefriars designs. These are now worth buying at between £20 and £50.

TOP TIPS

• Many of the lesser known Scandinavian artists signed their works. Even if the signature is unfamiliar, the fact that the piece is signed will still add value.

• Many English manufacturers produced examples that were quite similar to the Scandinavian designs. These are also worth collecting, with prices currently as cheap as £10.

• The size of a piece will not affect its value, but pieces with intricate designs or unusual shapes will generally be more valuable.

LOT 49: McDONALD'S TOYS

When McDonald's decided to hook up with Walt Disney and introduce a children's toy into each Happy Meal, they may not have realised that these toys would develop a following as collectors' items.

Ever since 1996, whenever a new Disney film came out you could guarantee that within two weeks, the plastic figures would be included and available at McDonald's in a Happy Meal package. Sometimes their release was spread over a couple of months, and one particular figure from the film was released each week. This, of course, meant that the collectors and their children would have to go back for more and more Happy Meals to build their collections. McDonald's, as always, was highly commercially minded, and themed boxes which matched the toy enclosed were also introduced.

The Disney toys are amongst the rarest early examples of McDonald's toys, but other toys pre-date the Disney examples. The first Happy Meal came out in 1979, and was called the Circus Happy Meal. It cost one US dollar and contained a McDoodler stencil, a puzzle book, a McWrist wallet, an ID bracelet and McDonaldland character erasers. Add the actual meal to that and today this seems like a pretty good bargain for a mere dollar!

Items to look out for

• The most desirable toys, regardless of age, are the Automata models, or those with moving arms or nodding heads. These must still be in their original polythene packaging in order to be catagorised as an investment for the future. Expect to pay a maximum of £20 for these items.

• For other models, packaging, design styles, colourways and country of origin will determine the price. Expect to pay £2–£4 for unpackaged items and £5–£10 for packaged items.

TOP TIPS

• Try to stick to a budget and a theme if possible. Collecting only the Disney characters, for example, should reap rewards one day, especially since Disney terminated its cross-promotional pact with McDonald's in 2006.

• A vast number of these toys have been thrown away, but many still do exist, so a collector can afford to be fussy.

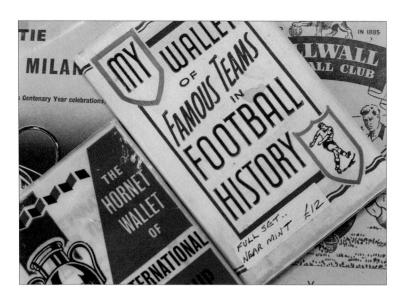

LOT 50: WORLD CUP MEMORABILIA 2006

Football memorabilia will always have a prominent place in the sporting collectors' market, and memorabilia from the 2006 World Cup is sure to gain in value very quickly in the marketplace.

The most sought-after sports collectables are those items that were only available at the venues where the matches were played, such as the match programmes. Of course the most prized programme will be that of the World Cup Final. Many thousands of these will have been produced and held on to, but, equally, many thousands will have been discarded already. Players' autographs naturally command a premium.

Items to look out for

Needless to say, the amount of memorabilia out there is staggering. So, to start a collection, you need to narrow your selection down to a price bracket.

• The likes of Wedgwood, Doulton & Coalport will no doubt have produced some limited edition items. Try to secure one of the earlier numbers. For example, number 20 of a limited edition of 500 will be worth more than number 498 of 500.

• Charity auctions are perfect for World Cup memorabilia. Footballers are usually very generous and donate signed shirts, boots and footballs. Signed team photographs are hotly contested, but can usually be picked up for under £500. Individual signed photographs go for £100–£1,000, depending on the player.

• If you were lucky enough to attend a World Cup game and you managed to pick up a poster advertising a match, you could be in the money. These are normally designed by top artists and graphic designers.

TOP TIPS

• When considering a limited edition item, ensure that edition is a one-off run, and that it will not be reproduced repeatedly, like some mail order companies tend to do.

• Many a World Cup programme turns up on an Internet auction site. Get hold of one, then attend a league match where some of the players that feature in the programme are playing and try to get them to sign your programme. This will at least triple the value of your programme. Some people actually make a living by doing this!

LOT 51: 1940s UTILITY FURNITURE

The Second World War left Britain with a serious timber shortage and a real need for basic furniture. The UK Board of Trade stepped in and introduced guidelines for designers which specified the amount and quality of materials they could use to create solid, hardworking items for the British public.

The leading utility designers were John Gloag, Herman Lebus and Gordon Russell. Together with the other members of the Board of Trade's Advisory Committee, they produced the Utility Furniture Catalogue of 1943.

The catalogue contained guidelines for making furniture for each room in the house. It specified that items had to be made with sturdy oak or mahogany, and with mortised and pegged joints. Handles and knobs had to be wood rather than metal as the latter was needed for the war effort.

In 1946, with the end of the war in sight, a design panel, headed by Russell, put together a new utility range, but this was less of a hit with the British public. 'Utility' had become associated with the deprivation of war; people now wanted to take advantage of newly avail-able post-war materials.

The design team had one last stab at making 'utility' a success, with the Scandinavian-influenced 'Diversified' range in 1949, but it was never put into production, and by 1952 the scheme was ended. However, its legacy is considerable: it established the principles of 'good design' and paved the way for the contemporary styles that followed.

Collectors have avoided utility furniture over the past 60 years because of its bad name, but the time is now right to snap it up.

Items to look out for

• Try to pick up a whole suite, and make sure you get matching chairs. Bedroom and dining room suites are still ridiculously underpriced at between £100 and £300.

TOP TIPS
• Ensure the maker's mark and model are stamped on each piece.
• A lot of utility furniture was made for the military. As the armed forces periodically revamp their quarters, this furniture is often discarded. Why not approach your local army or naval base and see if it has any unwanted items?

LOT 52: 1950s UTILITY FURNITURE

The 1950s was the age of the consumer, when the postwar boom brought tremendous changes in Britain's homes. The mood was 'out with the old and in with the new'. Open-plan living was introduced, and fitted kitchens and appliances were the new must-haves for the housewife of the day. Houses were smaller than pre-war homes so furniture had to be stackable, or light enough to move about easily. Trolleys, sofa beds and ironing boards are, not surprisingly, all 1950's inventions.

Utility furniture was the B & Q of the 1950s, mass produced on a huge scale, cheaply made and sold in its hundreds of thousands. Items ranged from bedroom suites and dining room suites to sideboards, kitchen units and kitchen tables and chairs. They were sold in budget high-street stores such as the Co-op, and customers would often pay for their chosen items in weekly instalments.

For our parents and grandparents, these pieces would have been the most prized and treasured items in their homes. Yet they came to be seen as bits of old plywood that needed to be burnt and thrown in the skip.

A lot of utility furniture from the 1950s was not particularly well made; in fact, it was rather thrown together. But there was a handful of designers and architects who really put a distinctive angle on this type of furniture, and even some of the mass-produced items are now collectable. Leading names from the period include Charles and Ray Eames, Robin and Lucienne Day and Arne Jacobsen. There were also plenty of 'unknowns' who copied the style of these masters – and this is where you should be looking for a bargain. Pieces by these lesser designers can be picked up relatively cheaply at auctions and antiques fairs.

Items to look out for
• Many coffee- and side-tables were made during this time. These are going for £10–£20.
• Free-standing kitchen pieces; most have coloured Formica fronts. These cost £40–£75.

TOP TIPS
• Research the period as carefully as you can by looking through style magazines, furniture catalogues and reference books

from the 1950s.
• Many items are recognisable in that they clearly have a Scandinavian minimalist influence.

LOT 53: PUNK ROCK

Punk rock was a short-lived but magical moment in the history of popular music which sent shock waves through society and inspired a generation of fashion designers and artists.

Punk originated with American bands like the Ramones and the New York Dolls. Malcolm Mclaren was largely responsible for bringing punk to the UK, and his shop, 'Sex', in London's King's Road, which he ran with fashion designer Vivienne Westwood, became the epicentre of the movement in England. In 1976 Mclaren formed a band, the Sex Pistols.

Punk music emphasized simple musical arrangements, accompanied by confrontational lyrics. Songs such as 'Career Opportunity' and 'London's Burning' by The Clash dealt with the grim realities of urban living at the time. Others openly attacked the monarchy, such as the Sex Pistols' 'God Save the Queen' and 'Anarchy in the UK'.

Punk fashion loved bold colours with ripped materials in tartan and stripes, studded leather jackets, mohair jumpers, black plastic skirts and bondage trousers. Extravagant body piercings and dramatic make-up complemented the look.

Items to look out for

• Early Sex Pistols albums from 1976. Expect to pay up to £60.
• Original clothing. Expect to pay up to £60.
• Singles and LPs from the period can cost between £4 and £40. Check the condition of the cover as well as that of the record. Graphic design on the cover, especially by a well-known artist, will enhance the price.
• Posters from the early punk rock period of the mid-70s will set you back £50–£200. The more obscure the band, the more prized the poster. Beware of reproductions.

TOP TIPS
• Any memorabilia from the Clash, Generation X or X-Ray Specs from 1976–80 will have some value to collectors.
• Try to find early posters, albums or singles.
• Seek out early American punk records and memorabilia from bands such as the Ramones, the New York Dolls and Television.
• Punk clothing, especially by Vivienne Westwood, is highly sought after. It is difficult to find and expensive, but it is a great investment if you are lucky enough to find it.

LOT 54: WADE POTTERY C.1950s

The Wade company was founded in 1887 and is still trading today. I believe 1950s Wade will be an important area for the collector over the coming years.

The Wade factory produced some of the most graphic pieces of pottery during the 1950s. Most of these are easily spotted by their strong use of colour, including stark black and white, bright red and strong yellow. These colours, together with the pottery's unusual fluid shapes and fashionable images, make Wade one of the best factories to collect for an authentic 1950s look. Furthermore, Wade pottery from the 1950s to '70s, despite having had a strong influence on the market at the time of its production, is overlooked by many Wade collectors, making these objects a prime target for a future collectable.

The 'Samba' range has bold decoration in black and white depicting tribal dancers. 'Samba' designs include ashtrays, jugs and unusually shaped vases.

Wade's 'Figural Cat' vases were typical of the period. Strong and highly graphic, the vase has four pronged feet and the interior is finished with red enamel. Many factories copied this footed shape, which was also reflected in the furniture of the day. As fashion moved on, however, these ornaments seemed old-fashioned and many were discarded.

Illustrated items by Rowland Emmet are also sought after by collectors. Emmet was a well-known cartoonist whose eccentric humour appealed to a wide audience. Most of his illustrations are on small Wade items, including coasters, ashtrays and pin cushions.

Items to look out for
• Samba vase for £30–£40. Samba ashtrays and other small items for £10–£15.
• Figural Cat vases. Expect to pay £50–£80 for a pair.
• Small pieces illustrated by Rowland Emmet. Expect to pay £5–£10.

TOP TIPS
• Unfortunately Wade's more unusual shapes are prone to hairline cracks, and the black enamel on the interior is prone to crazing and eventual peeling. It is therefore necessary to study the item carefully for signs of repainting.
• Check that the transfer on any illustrated piece has no scratching and is generally in good order.

LOT 55: ROYAL ACADEMY SUMMER EXHIBITION PAINTINGS AND PRINTS

The Summer Exhibition is held annually at the Royal Academy in London. A panel of nominated academicians chooses a small number of the many tens of thousands of paintings, prints, sculptures and other works that are shown at the Academy during the course of a year to feature in the exhibition. For many artists this represents the pinnacle of success. Some will try year in and year out and never manage to get their picture hung in the Summer Exhibition.

The Summer Exhibition stands out from most others because 90 percent of the works of art are actually for sale. They must remain in place for the duration of the exhibition, but once it is over they can be taken away by their new owners. The prices can range from £150 to a whopping £1,000,000.

Any artists that do make it into the exhibition naturally see the price of their art rise immediately. For example, a Victorian painting exhibited at the Summer Exhibition will command at least 40 percent more than a picture by the same artist which has not been exhibited. For this reason, you should make great efforts to secure a piece from the Summer Exhibition. As a footnote, my congratulations

go to Jim Moir, aka Vic Reeves, who had two pictures accepted for the Summer Exhibition of 2006. Buy his works now while they are still affordable!

Items to look out for

• Limited-edition prints, etchings and silk screen prints can be bought unframed for £100–£300. Go for one of the lower numbers if possible: one of the first 10 from a limited edition of 100, for example.

• Oil paintings and watercolours can cost anywhere from £300–£500,000, but the fact that these pictures have been exhibited at the Royal Academy will guarantee them a place in history.

TOP TIP
• It is worth paying an extra few pounds to secure an artist's proof (those prints reserved specifically for the artist). In a print run of 100, for example, the first 10 proofs are usually marked 'artist's proof.'

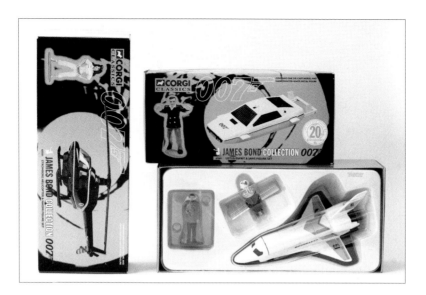

LOT 56: MODERN LIMITED EDITION TOYS

Dinky, Corgi and Matchbox are names dear to many a collector. The first toy cars date back to the early 1930s, when they were made by Hornby and known as 'modelled miniatures'. In 1933 the cars were given their own brand name, Dinky. This was without a doubt the golden age of the Dinky toy.

By the 1990s collecting Dinky toys and die-cast cars had reached its peak. Inevitably, Matchbox (who by then were the producers of Dinky) began to produce some limited edition models, and in 1991 the company decided to restrict their output and limit colour reissues in order to enhance collectability.

The company's ploy worked, and today's limited editions from that period can fetch anywhere between £20 and £40. Although the gain on these items will be relatively small, they are still worthy of investigation due to the fact that many are kept in pristine condition. The toys being produced today are also worth investing in.

The collectability of any toy car will depend upon its relative rarity, its shape, and the event it is commemorating. For example, in 2005 a 1,500-run limited edition of a Spitfire plane with a dog at its side, representing the famous George 'Grumpy' Unwin, sold out immediately and is already commanding a premium in the market.

Items to look out for

• Limited and special edition Matchbox toys from the 1990s are slowly gaining a place in the collectable toy market. Expect to pay £10–£40.
• Some of the most popular movies of the 1990s, along with television shows of this decade, have been reproduced in die cast models. Look out specifically for reproductions of the movie or show characters, as some are limited edition examples and are worth investing in.

TOP TIPS

• You can be sure that the more your initial investment in a limited edition toy, the better your return will be.
• Be sure to keep all packaging, receipts and any related ephemera in good condition.
• Look for toys made between 1990–2000, as these should prove to be a particularly good investment.

LOT 57: 20TH CENTURY NURSERY WARE

Nursery ware has been a favourite amongst British collectors since the 19th century. Items from the Art Deco period, especially those with designs by Mabel Lucie Attwell have enjoyed a longstanding popularity, as have the Royal Doulton Bunnykins pieces, designed by the artist Barbara Vernon Bailey in the 1930s and still in production today.

W. R. Midwinter Limited is another important nursery ware manufacturer from the 1930s. The company produced a range of wares decorated with 12 nursery rhymes after illustrations by William Heath Robinson. These are highly collectable.

I feel that future pickings in the nursery ware market will come from the 1980s to the present day. Popular cartoon characters, such as Rowland Rat from the 1980s, or the Telly Tubbies from the early years of 2000 should prove sound investments. The key is to keep your eyes open for current trends in children's television and books, even it if they appear to be passing fads. Short-lived characters can show as good a profit as established cartoon favourites like Mickey or Minnie Mouse.

Items to look out for

• Royal Doulton and Wedgwood are top factories, although you will pay more for their items as they generally produced their wares in smaller numbers. These companies often made limited edition pieces, which are good ones to look out for.

• Mable Lucy Attwell designed some tea sets and dinner services in miniature form, solely for dollhouses or for children's use. These are now worth £200–£400.

• Pre-1950s Bunnykins figurines that are marked with the name 'Barbara Vernon Bailey' included in the makers' back stamp on the base of the piece are highly prized by collectors. Expect to pay between £100–£200 depending on size and quality.

TOP TIPS

• As with all china and collectable porcelain, make sure that there is no damage or scratches on the item, and no evidence of restoration.

• Expect to pay more for nursery ware from Royal Doulton and Wedgwood, but these pieces are a good investment.

• Be sure to keep the original packaging when investing in modern nursery ware.

LOT 58: VHS VIDEOS AND RECORDERS

Technology, technology, technology – the mantra of the forward-thinking investor.
I am of the opinion that in the technology antiques market, the future is particularly
bright for certain video tapes and recorders.

In 1976, when the VHS video player first emerged, it would have set you back £798 (equivalent to a sum of £3,000 today). Yet in 2006 you can pick up a video recorder (admittedly at the bottom end of the market) for £34.97. To illustrate further how times have changed, the average weight of a video recorder in 1976 was 13.5kg (30 lb); today it is 1.8kg (4 lb).

At the height of its popularity in 1998, the video recorder graced 93 percent of British homes. Sales totalled 100,000,000, compared with just 200,000 for the newly introduced DVD players. The VHS itself had succeeded the old Betamax tapes, which in turn had succeeded the Philips VCR 2000 range. These earliest VCRs are highly sought after for their uniqueness and good quality.

Collecting VHS videos and video recorders allows you to be selective. Pick a type of video or recorder to concentrate on and stick with that target.

Items to look out for

• Invest in a VCR recorder that was expensive in its day and buy one of the top quality makes. Expect to pay £10-£50.
• When selecting tapes to collect, go for cult films, especially if they star modern-day Hollywood stars such as Keira Knightly, Tom Cruise, Brad Pitt, Leonardo di Caprio or Julia Roberts. Try sourcing these actors' very first movies and be sure that the tapes have their original packaging. These will cost £1-£3.

TOP TIPS

• It might be worth talking to your local video shop to see if you can have any film posters or other advertising paraphenalia that it no longer has use for. These items will make a nice addition to your video library, and can, with time, rise in price.

• Steer clear of ex-rental copies of tapes, as they have been viewed by many people and thus are probably worn out.
• If you find yourself at a flea market while on holiday abroad, it's worth looking for obscure titles that use English dialect, as these will add diversity to your collection.

LOT 59: PIN CUSHION DOLLS 1900-1950

Delicate and often ornately crafted, porcelain pin-cushion dolls were produced in their millions from the late 19th century to the 1950s. Since they require no special stands or cases, these little half dolls make an ideal collector's item for someone with limited space.

The pin cushion doll is comprised of two halves: the top half is the torso of a lady in period dress, whether Victorian, Art Deco or 50s, and the bottom half is the pin cushion itself, or a skirt designed to cover a teapot or powder box. At the base of each doll are four holes to attach the doll to the pin cushion itself. Some dolls are fully clothed, others partly clad and some even nude. Most measure between 8cm–12cm (3 in–5 in).

As with all collectables, there is a top end of the market and with pin cushion dolls it is the German models (some of which were even made by Dresden). Most models are marked with a maker or an incise mark with a number.

As is typically the case, with the vast amount of pin cushion dolls on the market, the collector can afford to be fussy.

Items to look out for
• Dolls from the top German factories such as Dresden and Miessen. Expect to pay £100–300.
• Dolls from other factories will go for £10–£40, depending on condition, style and profile.
• Art Deco dolls, especially those in the form of jewellery boxes with a half-doll top. Expect to pay £15–£60. Be prepared for large variations in quality.

TOP TIPS
• When checking for quality, look carefully at the doll's hands and fingers. The more realistic these are, the better the quality. This rule also applies to the quality of the painting on faces. Obviously, a lifelike face with portrait-quality features will be more valuable than a bland-looking face.

• Always check for evidence of restoration and for damage, and always take a spyglass with you when selecting your purchase.
• Search thoroughly for any chips or knocks to the piece, especially to the hands, nose or hair, as any damage to the piece will bring its value down.

LOT 60: NORITAKE PORCELAIN AND CHINA 1904-1985

Noritake china was first made in 1904 in the village of Noritake, a small suburb near Nagoya, Japan, by the Nippon Toki Kaisha factory. The initial goal of the company was to create the first porcelain dinnerware plate to be suitable for export. Today, Noritake has factories throughout the world, and is sold in over 100 countries.

The body of Noritake ware is a hard, white, translucent porcelain with delightful patterning. The ware is marked 'Noritake' and, if it entered England as a direct import, also bears the country of origin mark, 'Japan', 'Made in Japan' or 'Nippon'. Given that Noritake is exported all over the world, including to countries that do not have country of origin regulations, you will find plenty of pieces out there that have no additional markings. The earliest Noritake items were hand painted; now the artists' designs are transferred by decalcomania (the design is transferred from prepared paper onto another surface).

Noritake is often overlooked by collectors of pottery and porcelain because the word 'Japan' on the bottom of the ware implies mass production. This is a mistake – there are some exquisite individual pieces out there.

Items to look out for

• Single cabinet cups and saucers, particularly the early ones based on English styles and hand painted. Expect to pay between £80–£200 depending on the size and quality.

• Large Oriental-style vases marked 'Nippon' on the base. Try to buy pairs and expect to pay between £80 and £400, depending on the size, quality and decoration.

• Noritake produced and still produces many dinner services and tea sets. The quality is stunning and on a par with that of any English or German factory. Grossly underrated in auction rooms and at antique fairs, complete sets can be picked up for £200–£500.

• Afternoon tea sets comprising tea pot, milk jug, sugar basin and cream jug, with six or eight place settings, are also currently undervalued. Expect to pay £40–£120.

TOP TIP
• As always with porcelain or china, condition is critical. The rich blue background which was used on many of the sets of Noritake vases should be as vibrant as when it was new.

73

LOT 61: GUCCI HANDBAGS

The first Gucci handbag was born in a little shop in Florence over 70 years ago. It has been a symbol of style, sophistication, wealth and extravagance ever since.

The Gucci company grew from humble beginnings. Guccio Gucci developed a taste for beauty and elegance as a young man while working in London's affluent Savoy Hotel as a lift attendant. The son of a Florentine craftsman, he spent his early years between Paris and London, and it was from these international surroundings that he gained his sense of cosmopolitan style.

In the early 1920s, Guccio returned to Florence to open a leather goods shop, which started out selling luggage and saddlery. His reputation for high-quality craftsmanship, and in particular his horseriding accessories, first gained him fame. The shop produced the first Gucci handbag in the mid-1930s.

In the 1950s Gucci opened its first New York store and created the 'classic' Gucci items: the handbag with bamboo handles; the moccasin with the distinctive Gucci snaf-fle-bit; the foulards; the belt clasps; the ties.

The real explosion of the Gucci brand came in the 1960s, when the company opened stores all over the world. It was then that the brand became truly acknowledged as a status symbol; carrying a Gucci handbag meant that you were part of the in-crowd.

Items to look out for
• The resale value of vintage Gucci handbags remains good, so it's worthwhile trying to get hold of them. It's difficult to give exact prices for Gucci items – they will vary from £25 to £500, depending on the period and style.
• Do not be afraid to collect modern or contemporary styles. The company continues to offer new products and designs that have the same timeless appeal and sophistication as their classics, and these should hold their price well.

TOP TIPS
• Beware of fakes – they are absolutely everywhere! To recognise the real thing you will have to be prepared to do a bit of research and really familiarise yourself with the Gucci brand.
• Ask your friends and family if they own any Gucci items. You never know, someone might have an old item they no longer use or want.

LOT 62: PORTMEIRION 1960–1980

Susan Williams-Ellis and her husband, Euan, bought the world-famous Gray's pottery in Stoke-on-Trent in 1960, and this marked the start of Portmeirion pottery.

Susan began to design striking and original coffee and tableware, rather against the trend of the 1960s, which was to use black-and-white engravings of Victorian images. Her bold designs and unusual shapes made Portmeirion pottery as famous as the model village after which it was named. Among the many hugely successful Portmeirion lines were the 'Dolphin', 'Totem' and 'Tivoli' ranges.

The original Dolphin design was on a pink lustre background or a mix-and-match collection of Neapolitan colours. Due to the roaring success of the Dolphin pattern, the range was extended from storage jars to rolling pins, jugs and plates. The Dolphin design was updated towards the end of the 1960s and placed on vivid psychedelic mugs, which appealed to the younger generation.

Launched in 1963, the Totem range took the pottery market by storm. Portmeirion could not cope with the demand, and rival companies were soon cashing in with imitations. These could not, however, compete with the imaginative decoration of the originals.

Much of Susan's inspiration for her pottery came from her travels; for example, the Tivoli design was based on the Tivoli Gardens in Copenhagen. Formed as a screen print, this design was intended to be cut to fit any cylindrical shape.

Items to look out for

• Complete Tivoli coffee set in the Serif shape. Expect to pay £70–£120 for a six-place setting.
• Single pieces such as tankards, cream jugs and Dolphin spice jars. Expect to pay £2–£10.
• Any items from the Totem and Dolphin ranges. Single pieces cost between £10–£40, depending on size.

TOP TIPS

• The design of Tivoli coffee sets makes them prone to damage on the lids and the rims of the cups. Any damage to a single item will affect the value of the entire set.

• Portmeirion has an oval back stamp in the base, normally with the pattern included. Beware of an ochre-coloured stamp as this is a more recent addition and has been used on seconds.

LOT 63: FISHING LURES

The next time you're rummaging through the garden shed it's worth taking a long, hard look at that old tackle box. Fishing lure collectors have driven the price of pre-1940 lures by famous manufacturers and in un-fished condition through the roof. Even some of the 1940s to late 1960s plastic lures are now bringing in excess of £40 each.

Antique lures (1890-1930) are hot collecting items. It almost seems as if anyone who collects anything is looking for old lures, and the most sought after are the fly-fishing type. Of course, we're not talking about those lures with teeth marks all over the body and paint chipped off, but rather the ones the owner has kept on the shelf as a back-up or has put away in a box. In the world of antique lures, condition is everything.

Generally, the most collectable lures were produced by the major companies, such as Hardy. But don't ignore old lures made by some of the more obscure companies that may not have been in business for longer than a year (and who produced their lures during the period 1910–1930). These lures can also bring big money to the lucky seller.

Fishing accessories from the 1940s to the '70s are also big news these days. The lure boxes, reels, trout creels, fly rods, old fishing displays from hardware or sporting goods stores and even the gizmo-type gadgets are highly prized.

Items to look out for

• Single fishing lures from 1890-1930. These cost anywhere from £25–£75.
• Fishing lures from the 1960s and '70s. These are grossly underrated by collectors at the moment, and most makes will eventually show a profit – the more elaborate, the better. Depending on their condition, these can be had for anywhere between £10–£40.

TOP TIPS

• Ask friends and family if they have any old lures or fishing accessories hidden away in the garden shed. You never know – you could get lucky.

• Sometimes old shop displays advertising lures for sale will have several lure samples housed in a glass cabinet. These displays can be worth a whopping £500-£1,000 if you manage to find one.

LOT 64: MODERN BRITISH FURNITURE DESIGNERS – SIR TERENCE CONRAN AND ERNEST RACE

Two of the hottest names in the current furniture collecting market are Sir Terence Conran and Ernest Race. Sourcing their designs, especially the originals, will almost certainly reap a profit. You'll find the entry level for some items to be quite high, but there are still pieces to be had for less than £100.

The 1960s and '70s witnessed a new style of furniture-retailing in Britain, and Terence Conran and his Habitat stores were the leaders in the field. Influenced by a visit he had made to Europe in the 1950s, Conran began a furniture retailing revolution. He started by grouping furniture together in lifestyle formats and areas, and complementing these with fixtures and fittings. His aim was to create an exciting living area within the store which could be transported to a buyer's home.

Ernest Race is a little known but very influential British furniture designer who worked from the 1940s onwards, making furniture from materials which were remnants of the Second World War. Race also largely pioneered the use of steel rod frame construction for seating furniture.

Items to look out for
• A wicker chair on metal hairpin legs, based on an Eames design from the 1960s. Expect to pay £80–£120.
• Early pine pieces by Conran from Habitat c.1960s. A chest of drawers can be had for about £150; a side table for around £75.
• An Ernest Race-designed steel and plywood Antelope chair, originally designed for the Festival of Britain in 1951. Expect to pay £200–£300.
• A 1950s white-painted metal rod rocking chair by Race. Expect to pay £200–£400.

TOP TIPS
• It may seem obvious, but always make sure that any item you're considering is attributed to the designer in question.

• Many Race items are designed for use outdoors, so make sure you bring them inside over the winter months if you want them to retain their value.

LOT 65: CONTEMPORARY DESIGNERS – PHILIPPE STARCK AND RON ARAD

During the 1980s a number of designers began to make a name for themselves by creating modern furniture and kitchen appliance designs in limited editions. Two of the best known designers from this time are Ron Arad and Philippe Starck.

Philippe Starck's unique designs fit into any contemporary living space. His range is extraordinary – he has put his inimitable stamp on everything from toothbrushes and kettles to doorknobs, luggage and office furniture. He is also very well known for designing some of the most popular hotels in the world, including the Clift Hotel in San Fransisco and New York's Hudson Hotel. Ron Arad is best known for his 'art' furniture chairs, including the Big Easy Red chair. He has also designed a wide variety of objects for many high-profile design companies, including Alessi, Artemide, Kartell and Vitra.

Both Arad and Starck succeeded in developing their own names into brands, and I am one hundred percent confident that their designs will go on to become great classics. Recently, a set of four Ed Archer chairs and an end table, designed by Philippe Starck for Driade from around 1986, sold at auction for £1,200 – hardly more than you would pay for an average contemporary set without the designer name.

At present many items are at a premium, but superb examples of designs from Starck and Arad's early work often turn up in second-hand furniture stores. These are the pieces you should be looking out for.

Items to look out for
• Philippe Starck's work does not have to be expensive. There is a Starck-designed fly swat currently on the market for a mere £6.
• At the other end of the market, some Starck furniture from the early 1980s can set you back between £500–£700.
• Keep your eyes open for Alessi pieces designed by Arad; these will go for £40–£50. A chair by Arad can be had for £100–£150.

TOP TIP
• If you want to collect Starck and Arad, the first rule is to do your research. This will help you feel confident enough to spot a fake. Keep in mind that both of these designers marked or signed their works.

LOT 66: KEITH MURRAY FOR WEDGWOOD

When Joshua Wedgwood & Sons decided to commission New Zealand-born architect Keith Murray to design a range of affordable, mass-produced pottery items in the 1930s, they gained themselves a look that was ahead of its time. Simple yet stylised, Murray's striking pottery made its dramatic entrance while many other potteries were closing down.

Keith Murray had already established his reputation as a glassware designer for Stevens & Williams. Although the Wedgwood-Murray combination was initially slow to kick in, by 1933 other designers had started to sit up and pay attention to his new approach. Murray's work from this period is instantly recognisable: a sleek design with matt glazes, usually coloured green or straw. Rarer examples also exist in grey, blue and black basalt.

Three different back stamps were used over the years. The first, from 1933, was a form of the Murray signature. By 1934 the mark had been shortened to 'KM', and by 1940 the stamp was the initials 'KM' and the words of 'Etruria' (the area of Stoke-on-Trent where Wedgwood was based).

Items to look out for

• Simple shapes, such as the plain ovoid vase with a strong, clean, ribbed design. Expect to pay £300–£500.

• A desk tray, produced between 1933 and 1937. Few were made and even fewer have survived intact. Trays with a glaze by Norman Wilson can fetch up to £1,500 at auction.

• More affordable items include tableware such as a cream jug with moonstone glaze and silver lustre highlights for £30–£50; and a sugar bowl and lid in the same range for £80–£100.

• Black basalt ranges are the most valuable (and are often undersold by traders and dealers). A 12-cm (5-in) high black basalt vase will cost £1,200–£1,500.

TOP TIPS

• Check carefully for chips. The tiniest flaw and the price will plummet.
• Seek out the rarer colours, such as the greys and blues and the black basalt.

• Beware of fakes. Murray's work is always clearly marked on the base and his shapes were listed in the Wedgwood shape book. The first pattern number is 3,753 and the last is 4,326.

LOT 67: BUBBLE CARS

In the 1950s there was nothing on the roads quite as unique as the bubble car. This innovative little car came into its own after the Second World War, when many people could not afford a larger vehicle.

The bubble car was the brainchild of Italian designer Renzo Rivolta, who entered the UK market with a line of scooters, motorcycles and three-wheel trucks. After some success, he decided to move on to automobiles.

The first Renzo-designed car was the Iso in 1952-1953; it was a mere 1.35m (1½ yds) wide and 2.25m (2½ yds) long. It had a single door to the front and claimed to be able to do 80km (50 miles) to the gallon (4.5L). It was run on a two-stroke engine and had a top speed of 75kmph (45 mph). The Iso's success caught the eye of BMW who, at the time, was producing cars that few could afford. In 1955 Isetta sold BMW a license to make the car, and the first model appeared later that year.

In 1957 Britain began producing its own bubble cars at a Brighton-based factory, 'Isetta of Great Britain Ltd'. The original four-wheel model proved unpopular, and a three-wheel model was introduced. This was better received, partly, no doubt, because the three-wheel car was taxed at a lower rate than four-wheelers at the time.

By the early 1960s the Mini had made its dramatic entrance, and in 1962, production of the three-wheel bubble car came to a halt.

The Isetta was the most successful of the bubble cars – BMW actually built over 140,000 of them; Isetta of Great Britain around 30,000. Of the 8,500 exported to the USA there are reputedly 1,000 still in existence.

Items to look out for

• Bubble cars are not cheap. Expect to pay £3,000–£7,000, depending on condition, originality, mileage, model and colour. Whatever your outlay, you can expect a good return.

TOP TIPS

• If you find an example you want to buy, be sure the service history and full documentation are attached.

• If you are interested in bubble cars, visit the National Bubble Car Museum in Lincolnshire, UK, to see a great collection of 1950s–60s micro and bubble cars.

• The Internet and vintage-car magazines are good places to source bubble cars.

LOT 68: MOBILE PHONES

I can hold my hand up and say that I did once own the house brick, as we call it now, more commonly known then as the Motorola 8500X Etacs. I can remember my wife and I going to London and arguing over who was going to carry it. After two calls the batteries would go dead, so we always had to carry a spare battery as well as the phone, and airtime was almost as expensive as the phone itself. Ah, the heady days of 1990!

t is hard to imagine that it was only in 1982 hat mobile phones came into public use. The Motorola 8500X was released in the late 1980s, and cost £200–£300. Thankfully, technology has advanced steadily since that time, and many mobile phones have been made and discarded as technology has quickly replaced itself – and continues to do so at a dizzying pace.

The true boom in mobile phones didn't really happen until the late 1990s. By concentrating on the pre-1995 models, therefore, you will be investing in a future collectable. These are the models I think you should look out for.

Items to look out for
• Swedish Erickson EH97. Look for a sample from 1992–1994 with a flip-up aerial. Expect to pay £10–£30.
• Motorola Etacs personal phone; this unusual model has no LCD or digital display. Released in 1992 for £250, it is worth £20–£50 today.
• Sony CM-DX1000. Known as the Mars Bar phone, it had a sliding earpiece and an extending aerial. Produced in 1995 and rare today. Expect to pay £60–£90.
• Nokia 101 Etacs and the Nokia 2110 GSM will each cost £20-£30.

TOP TIPS
• Always check that the battery is original.
• If the phone has a retractable aerial, make sure this still works.
• Camshell phones, in which the earpiece folds over the keyboard, were more popular abroad than in Britain. Some of the British examples will thus become collectors' items.
• Pre-2000 phones produced for famous films or events are worth keeping an eye out for.
• Seek out examples in unusual colours, including simulated woods.

LOT 69: STUART DEVLIN SILVER

Modern silver is a great area to invest in at the moment, and Stuart Devlin is a one of the most acclaimed and skilled 20th-century silver designers. His work is more affordable than that of most well-known 18th- and 19th-century silversmiths.

Stuart Devlin was born in Geelong, Australia, in 1931. He originally wanted to become an art teacher, but he soon realised that precious metals were his forte, and in 1957 he began studying at Melbourne College for a Diploma of Art in gold and silversmithing. In the late 1950s, on the strength of his work at Melbourne he gained a scholarship to study at the Royal College of Art in London. In 1965 he opened a small workshop in London. His work from these early days marked the beginning of the 'Devlin style', as he moved away from the Bauhaus and Scandinavian designs that had influenced his earlier work to a more romantic use of precious metals.

Devlin believed that the role for a contemporary silversmith was to enrich the way people lived and worked. He felt that the craft of silversmithing, combined with the romantic nature of precious metals, gave him an opportunity to design items that added novelty,

intrigue and even humour to a discipline that had become somewhat austere.

He continued to work out of studios in London throughout the late 1960s and '70s and in 1982 he was granted the Royal Warrant of Appointment as Goldsmith and Jeweller to Her Majesty the Queen.

Some of Devlin's most popular commissions have been coins, which he has now designed for over 36 countries throughout the world. In addition, he has made commemorative medallions, furniture, jewellery, trophies, clocks and centrepieces, all of which are highly sought after by collectors.

Items to look out for
• Small silver boxes with hallmark dates to 1974. Expect to pay between £600–£900.
• Small trinkets such as letter-openers from the late 1970s. Expect to pay between £100–£200.

TOP TIP
• Try to pick up novelty Devlin items such as the Silver Clown Egg, the Silver Tortoise Egg or the Silver Kangaroo Egg. These are all limited editions, and thus are sure to rise in price.

LOT 70: BROADHURST & KATHIE WINKLE

Broadhurst may not be the most well-known name in pottery, even for collectors of 1950s and '60s pieces, but it is a significant one, particularly in terms of its association with the designer Kathie Winkle.

While the Broadhurst name may not have been as well known as those of other potteries, its output was by no means small. In fact, its most popular pattern, Rushstone, sold in excess of 55 million pieces.

Many pottery factories in the 1950s and '60s decided to put their designers' names on the back stamps of their wares. This was an ingenious idea – not only did it raise the profile of the company, but it made it seem designer orientated, too. Broadhurst followed the trend by adding the name of its in-house designer, Kathie Winkle, in 1964.

Kathie Winkle joined the Broadhurst Company in 1950. She produced her first design for the factory, a pattern called 'Perdo', in 1958. The two patterns that truly epitomise Kathie Winkle, however, are Capri and Corinth. Both of these designs have a small band of decoration to the edge of the item.

The Winkle pottery was created with a mixture of machine- and hand-crafted techniques. A stamping machine was used to transfer an image onto the plates and bowls, and the painter then added the coloured details to lift the design.

Teapots and coffee pots are among Kathie Winkle's most distinctive pieces. Among them are the Delta/Rivera range – a clever design with a small border which allowed the machine decoration to come into play – and the Electra range, first produced in 1969.

Items to look out for

• Teapots, coffee pots and serving items such as gravy jugs and cream jugs. These are not easy to find. Expect to pay £10–£20.

• Other Broadhurst patterns, including Tyne c.1961 and Calypso Bermuda c.1960–62. Such patterns were inexpensive and fresh in their time, and many were only produced for a short period. Expect to pay £2–£4 per item.

TOP TIP

• Many of Kathie Winkle's designs had simple borders, but she also created all-over patterns and it is these latter items which I feel have a particularly promising future in the collector's market.

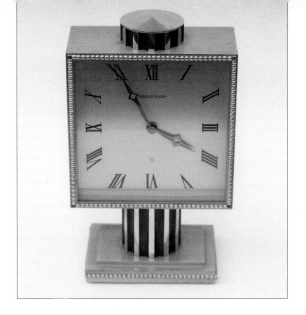

LOT 71: MANTLE CLOCKS 1940–1970

As early as the 18th century, clocks were placed on brackets or mantles to display as a feature in the home. Today, mantle clocks from the 18th and 19th centuries continue to adorn the mantles of homes throughout the world.

Mantle clocks from the 1940s to the '70s, however, seem to have slipped by many a clock collector, and thus this is the area in which I can see profitable returns in the coming years. Clocks from the Art Deco period in particular are usually pounced upon when they turn up in salerooms.

Items to look out for
• At the top end of the market, manufacturers and retailers such as Cartier, Jaeger LeCoultre and Japy Freres also produced mantle clocks, and their quality and craftsmanship make these clocks highly collectable. These makers also produced smaller versions of the mantle clocks known as desk clocks. Depending on size and clock movement, these will cost £150–£500.
• At the middle point in the market, look out for strong shapes and designs such as boat-shaped clocks or clocks in the form of a ship's

wheel. Some of these versions can also be used as wall clocks. Expect to pay between £15 and £40.
• At the budget end of the market, keep your eyes open for clocks made from plastic, simulated wood or Bakelite. One of the best-known makers of clocks in these materials is Metamec, whose battery-powered examples often come in vivid colours such as pink or red. Some of Metamec's designs are plain and simple, others are more stylised, but all are affordable at between £5 and £15.
• The Swiss maker Jaeger LeCoultre is one of the top names in mantle clocks and a clock with its name on it will cost between £300 and £3,000. If you have a healthy budget I would recommend investing in Jaeger LeCoultre's Atmos clock.
• Electric mantle clocks were a passing fad in the 1900–40s; many were shaped like classical clocks. These can cost up to £1,000.

TOP TIPS
• Source your collection based on the principles of style, design and maker.
• The better the clock movement, the more valuable the clock will be. A faulty mechanism will devalue the piece.

LOT 72: ALARM CLOCKS

Some of the alarm clocks from the 1950s, '60s and '70s boasted unusual yet delightful designs, serving their purpose with a large, loud ring. I feel that these items are soon to have their day amongst collectors.

Wacky, attractive and colourful sums up the alarm clocks made from the 1950s to the '80s. The cases and dials were made with the sole purpose of attracting the user's attention. Many alarm clocks from this period have a wind-up action; some are on stands, while others were made to be hung on the wall. Well known manufacturers include Smith's, Westclox, General Electric, Braun and Bulova.

Items to look out for

• It is worth keeping an eye out for digital electric bedside alarm clocks. Manufacturers like Braun mass-produced this type of clock, and they have been discarded over the years.

They can now be picked up for anywhere between £5–£20.
• Alarm clocks with pendulum-style second hands. These can be had for £5–£15.
• Cartoon or comic-orientated clocks pre-1970 are both good additions to an alarm clock collection, and can be had for £10–£15.
• Space-age design plastic clocks, alarm or mantle, from the 1960s to the '70s. Whether Continental or English, these clocks really typify the period. They are still available at between £20–£50.
• Tin-plate alarm clocks with automata action or unusual alarm bells from 1940–50 will cost up to £75.

TOP TIPS

• Amassing an alarm clock collection from the period 1950-70 would look stunning in any show cabinet. It would also show the progression of design through three decades, thus becoming a historical record of alarm clocks. Given time (ha ha), such a collection will definitely rise in value.
• The maker's mark on an alarm clock is not always instantly visible. Removing the back cover will often reveal the maker.
• Rewiring older electrical clocks will not devalue them. On the contrary, rewiring them will make them safer to use.
• A clock in its original box is worth more than an example without its original packaging.

LOT 73: STAINLESS STEEL DOMESTIC KITCHEN WARE

Often overlooked by collectors, the strong, stylised look of stainless steel makes it a must for collectors looking for retro-style future antiques.

Stainless steel domestic kitchen ware is in fact a 20th-century invention. It arrived on the market by accident around 1928, when a certain Mr and Mrs Wiggins were about to celebrate their silver wedding anniversary. Mrs Wiggins was ahead of her time, and requested something more practical than solid silver. At the time, her husband was running the firm J&J Wiggins, which specialised in stainless steel bathroom fittings, and so his gift to her was a stainless steel toast rack, the very first domestic stainless steel kitchen item.

Mr Wiggins soon realised that he might have hit on something, and soon after he formed the Old Hall Staybrite company, which produced the first stainless steel domestic items. While the company's earlier pieces were not stunningly designed, they do represent a significant moment in the short life of stainless steel.

The Old Hall Staybrite designs picked up during the 1950s, when Wiggins employed the designer Robert Welch, who designed some stunning pieces for the company.

Other countries also began to make kitchen ware from stainless steel, including Scandinavia and Italy. Significant Scandinavian producers included Stelton and Georg Jensen. In Italy, Alessi has specialised in stainless steel manufacturing since the 1950s, and continues to do so today.

Items to look out for
• Any Old Hall Staybrite designs by Robert Welch, including nut crackers (£60), cutlery sets (£25), and tea sets (£200).
• Early toast racks c.1930–50. These will cost 50p–£5.
• 1950s boxed cutlery by known designers. This will cost £15–£30.
• Cruet sets in unusual shapes (spear or oblong). These can be had for £4–£8.

TOP TIP
• In the late 1960s Arne Jacobsen designed a range for Stelton called 'Cylinda'. It is still possible to find items in this range in charity shops for under £20, but collectors will pay up to £300.

86

LOT 74: GEOMETRIC TREENWARE 1950-1970

Treenware is a generic term dating back to the 18th century that is used to describe small decorative wooden items. My specific tip for the collector is to buy geometric treenware from the 1950s and '60s, particularly bar and kitchen items. These are instantly recognisable and fairly plentiful as many homes of the period would have owned at least one piece of treenware.

Treenware was originally made by craftsmen who, working in major cities, used their wood offcuts to make pieces that they subsequently sold off to tourists. The craftsmen took exotic woods such as ebony, walnut, yew and blonde oak and cut them into small rectangular shapes. They then glued these shapes to the exterior of the base wood to form a geometric pattern. Each piece was finished off with a lacquered brass carrying handle and a solid-turned wooden lid. There was also a high end to this market based on exotic imported woods, especially Lignum Vitae, with which items were made for the wealthy.

Widely produced in both the UK and Europe, treenware is plentiful, although much of it has been discarded over the years.

Items to look out for

• Quirky items such as tobacco boxes, matchbox holders, letter racks and pen racks. These examples are not always easy to find, but they are affordable at £10–£15.

• Figurines produced by European firms, who realised the gains to be made from their offcuts of wood. Again, tricky to find, but worth it. Expect to pay £25–£40.

• Practical items such as ice buckets or biscuit barrels. Expect to pay £8–£15, but ensure that the original china liner (the lining inside the barrel) is intact.

• Carved animals. Often called 'Black Forest' items because of the origin of the wood used (the Black Forest in Germany), smaller items cost £60; larger items can reach up to £3,000.

TOP TIP

• If the item looks a bit grubby, don't let yourself be put off. This is usually just household grime or nicotine, and is easy to remove with a light soapy water mix followed by a coat of good furniture wax. Do not immerse the wood in the water; rather, wipe the piece gently with a cloth.

LOT 75: LIFE-SIZE CARDBOARD CUT-OUTS

Cardboard cut-outs are throwaway items made purely to advertise a film or an important event. I admit this may seem a rather eccentric tip for investment, but because they are one-offs, these items have the potential to become collectable.

Strange as it may sound, I believe that in 20 years or so there will be a strong market for cardboard cut-outs. They are, for all intents and purposes, works of art! Depending on how popular the subject, production is often relatively limited. Examples made to promote a one-off event are almost guaranteed not to have been reproduced, which alone makes this a good area to collect.

Items to look out for
• Cut-outs promoting major sporting events. Prior to and during the 2006 World Cup, life-size David Beckhams, Wayne Rooneys and Michael Owens became familiar sights at supermarkets and department stores, perched next to their sponsored merchandise.

• Famous Disney characters, usually produced over the Christmas period or to promote a new film. Their shelf life is normally quite short, so their condition is usually good.
• Video stores are a good source for the collector. I remember going into my local video-rental store when the film Titanic had just been released on video and my daughter had developed a crush on Leonardo di Caprio. At the front door stood a life-size Leo, which she desparately wanted. I asked whether we could keep the cut-out when it was done with, and the clerk replied that he had been asked hundreds of times for it, and so he was putting it in a charity auction. As it turned out, I was the charity's auctioneer, and I ended up buying it for my very happy daughter for £50.

TOP TIPS
• Make sure you know the video release date of the film or event – that way you can be first in line at your local store.
• It's worth making a small donation to charity to secure the cut-out. Between £15 and £20 is normally sufficient.

• Approach the film's distributors. They might even have a back catalogue you could choose from.
• Try to find characters associated with unusual or cult films, as these will be more rare and thus more valuable.

LOT 76: POUL HENNINGSEN PH LAMP

Scandinavian designers have given us many modern classics, yet few pieces have achieved the iconic status of the Poul Henningsen PH lamp, recognised throughout the world and still refreshingly affordable.

Poul Henningsen was born in Denmark in 1894. He initally trained as an architect, but he soon became fascinated with the exciting new technology of the electric light bulb, and decided to dedicate himself to producing striking and innovative light fittings. His aim in designing light fittings was to recreate the soft gas lighting effect he had known as a child (Henningsen's home town had had no electricity when he was growing up).

Henningsen experienced early success in his collaboration with Louis Poulsen & Co, a firm which sold tools and electrical supplies. Together, Henningsen and the firm sought to develop a lamp that they could enter into the modern lighting section of the Paris Exposition Internationale des Arts Décoratifs et Industriels Modernes of 1925.

Henningsen's design, known as the PH lamp, ended up taking first prize at the Exposition. Based on scientific studies of light and shade distribution, the lamp was designed specifically to avoid glare. The PH design proved commericially successful, and Henningsen expanded his range of lamps. Within a few years of the launch of the original PH lamp, many Scandinavian homes and institutions could boast a Henningsen-designed lamp shade.

Items to look out for

• The original PH lamp shade. Expect to pay £250 for a new one. Another option is to buy one second-hand; expect to pay around £65.
• Henningsen's majestic artichoke lamp shade, produced in 1958. It is composed of leaf-like elements and, with its grand size, is ideal for larger settings. It is almost as expensive as it is beautiful, however. Expect to pay £1,000–£1,500.

TOP TIPS
• eBay is the best place to look for a second-hand PH lamp shade. I recently secured one for £65.

• Rewiring the lamp will not affect its value, and will make it safer to use. Try to use authentical-style wire, though!

LOT 77: BUTTONS

Antique buttons are fantastic items for collectors. They are currently inexpensive, yet each small example is a work of art, often made by a superb craftsman.

Buttons have a long and fascinating history, and have been made from myriad materials over the centuries. In the 16th century, they were made from gilded silver, with their faces typically moulded in relief with patterns such as dragons, flowers or cupid's heads.

The 17th century saw buttons made from solid brass. These were soon pronounced too heavy for use on garments, however, and by 1680 they were replaced by tin examples with brass fronts.

The bizarre law that stated that buttons had to be made from precious metals was lifted in 1740. Pewter and silver soon became the fashion, along with brass and gilt. Steel, silver plate and iron were used from 1750-90; these buttons were often highly decorated.

The 19th century was a proud time to be a button-maker, with many manufacturers impressing their names onto their buttons.

Steel was now the fashionable material, and samples were highly decorated. By 1840 button styles changed once again, with filigree, Florentine silk, glass, pearl, and tortoiseshell all favoured by the leading button-makers.

Items to look out for

• Seventeenth- and 18th-century buttons. Expect to pay £3–£6 for single buttons; £100–£200 for boxed sets.

• Late 19th- and early 20th-century buttons made from carnelian, enamel, jet, pottery, porcelain, mother-of-pearl or glass, especially *millefiori*. Expect to pay 50p to £25 for single buttons, depending on the material; £50–£250 for boxed sets.

• Nineteenth-century jet buttons produced as a mark of respect during Queen Victoria's mourning for Prince Albert. These cost a mere £2–£3 each.

TOP TIPS

• Top button hunting grounds include second-hand clothes shops, junk shops and boot fairs.

• If the buttons are in their original boxes,

this will enhance their collectability.

• Many collectors look for a back mark, which helps to date the button. Look out for the maker's name, too.

LOT 78: LUDWIG MIES VAN DER ROHE, 1886-1969

Investing in a piece of furniture by German Art Deco legend Mies van der Rohe is a serious move, and will take out a good chunk of your bank balance. But if you are feeling bold, you could see a major return when selling.

The doyen of the modernist approach to furniture, Mies van der Rohe was a leading exponent of the Bauhaus machine-age philosophy, famous for the dictum 'less is more'. He was also a leading architect, creator of internationally renowned buildings such as the Barcelona Pavillion, the New National Gallery in Berlin and the Seagram Building in Manhattan.

From 1927 to 1931 Mies van der Rohe's furniture designs were manufactured by the company Berliner Metallgewerbe Joseph Müller, and after 1931 by Bamberg Metallwerkstätten. His furniture combines both classical and modernist elements, and achieves a machine-made look but with the luxury of a hand-made finish.

Mies van der Rohe's most famous creation is without doubt the Barcelona Chair. Created in 1929 for the World Exhibition in Barcelona, this iconic chair is still one of the most popular in the world, mass produced until well after the Second World War and still in production today. He also designed, in the same style, a Barcelona daybed, love seat, sofa, two- and three-seater benches and a coffee table. Contemporary imitations of these pieces are now produced by the furniture company Knoll International, which now has the exclusive rights to manufacture the Barcelona design.

Items to look out for

• Original Barcelona chairs from the early years (c. 1929-47). These cost around £10,000–£15,000 for the chair and around £2,000–£3,000 for the matching footstool.
• Knoll-produced Barcelona chairs. These cost £3,000–£3,500; £1,000-£1,500 for the matching footstool.

TOP TIPS

• The first Barcelona chairs produced were unstamped and had no makers mark.
• Always look for original upholstery, as this will be a major influence on price.
• In the USA and Germany it is actually illegal to call a chair a Barcelona Chair unless it is produced by Knoll.

LOT 79: BETTY JOEL

A number of British designers tried to bring the glamour of 1930s Hollywood to home-grown interiors, and Betty Joel was arguably the most successful of these. Imposing and solid-looking, yet with gently curved contours, Betty Joel furniture currently commands high prices that look set to climb higher still.

Born in Hong Kong, Betty Joel moved to England and set up a modest furniture warehouse in Hayling Island, near Portsmouth, in the early 1930s. Her first designs had an Arts and Crafts feel to them, but she soon became more influenced by French Art Deco styles. It wasn't long before her furniture was selling from exquisite showrooms in London's Knightsbridge.

Much of Joel's work was done on commission, typically for exclusive corporate or domestic buildings and equally exclusive clients, among them Louis Mountbatten and the then Duchess of York. She also produced deluxe works for decorator Syrie Maugham. Her furniture was usually built in as part of the dwelling, and so remained a fixture of the home or office. Her pieces were always hand-finished and her craftsmanship was excellent, with drawers fitting so perfectly that a gush of

air rushes out when the drawer is closed.

Joel eventually bucked the Art Deco trend and began to use luxury woods such as ebony, preferring grained woods arranged to achieve an almost monochromatic effect. Many items were finished with chromed steel to the plinths, curving around the piece almost like a female form. Most, if not all, of her works are well documented, and some pieces carry the label 'made at the Token Works, Kingston'.

Items to look out for

• Joel-designed armchairs (£3,500); side tables (£1,500) and footstools (£750 and up).
• The price for Joel originals may be prohibitive for most pockets but her designs and styles inspired many smaller cabinet-makers from the Art Deco period, whose furniture you should be able to source for between £500 and £2,500.

TOP TIP

• One good piece of Art Deco furniture will make a bigger statement than a series of smaller items – try to buy a piece that will act as a centrepiece or talking point.

LOT 80: NOVELTY CRUET SETS

Cruet sets are small, often intricate and delicate, containers designed to hold salt, pepper, mustard, oil and vinegar. Think of virtually any form or design and you can guarantee that a cruet set has been made to represent it. Compact and easy to display, cruet sets remain one of the most popular collector's items today.

I suggest that you start your collection of novelty cruets by concentrating on the period 1890–1910, and work your way through to 1990. This way you will build up a knowledge of the changing trends throughout the history of cruet-making.

The entry level for cruet-set collectors can be as little as £2–£4. Among the most popular pieces are those by the established factories of Carlton, Royal Doulton and Worcester. Clarice Cliff and Susie Cooper also produced some stunning examples; investing in these top names will always bring good returns.

Items to look out for
• A Carlton cruet set of vegetables modelled on a small leaf-like tray from the 1950s. Expect to pay £30–£50.

• Other Carlton ware novelty cruets, such as the mushroom-style cruet and the salad-style cruet featuring a tomato and a cucumber. Both of these sets can be bought for £30–£50.

• A Clarice Cliff 'Crocus' single cruet set – expect to pay £100–£150. For the 'Red Roof' pattern expect to pay £200–£500.

• A Susie Cooper novelty cruet set in a polka-dot pattern. Expect to pay £80–£100.

• Animal-shaped sets modelled as a group of animals. These will cost £15–£30.

• Sets shaped like cartoon characters or characters from films. Expect to pay £12–£40.

• Sets that are a singular shape but separate in to single cruets. Known as mystery cruets, they cost £20–£40.

TOP TIPS
• Check that the item is well-painted, and check also for any damage or restoration, as this will lower the set's value.

• With cruet sets from the 1900–1920s, ensure that the china stand is present.

• If you are holidaying in Europe, look out for the more unusual Continental cruet sets, which tended to be made in different styles than those found in the UK.

• Try to buy a set that represents the period in which it was made.

LOT 81: PHONE CARDS

Collecting old phone cards has been one of the fastest growing hobbies of the past ten years, with over five million collectors worldwide. I feel sure that this pursuit will one day be in the same league as stamp collecting.

The first phone card was issued in 1976, and today over 200 countries use these pre-paid cards, which are sold in small plastic packets.

As with many collectables, the most unusual cards will always be the most sought after. Anything which commemorates an event or a certain moment in history will be a short-lived edition and therefore highly prized.

It's up to you to decide which price range and types of cards you want to specialise in, but once you have made this decision, stick to it. Furthermore, as with any collectable, there is a great deal to learn about phone cards – do your research and you'll be better placed to make money in the market.

Items to look out for

• Early first-edition cards are a great place to start a collection, as they are readily available on Internet forums. Expect to pay £2–£10, irrespective of which country they come from.

• The introduction of mobile phones has almost annihilated the phone card business, but it is still surviving, if barely. It thus might be worth looking at the current phone cards on the market as future collectables. As more people acquire mobile phones, these cards will become increasingly scarce, and thus more valuable to collectors.

• Phone cards designed to commemorate occasions or holidays. Expect to pay £2–£10.

TOP TIPS

• Narrow down the range of your collection by choosing cards from specific years. For example, concentrate on pre-1990 cards to start with, then move on to 1990–1995, etc.

• Try to build a collection based around face values of the cards. Keep in mind that as the card value increments rise, the decoration on the card will also change.

As a rule, the higher the increment value on the card, the more the card will be worth

• There are many websites set up for phone card collectors. Here a few good ones: www.moneycard.com, www.leo-card.com, www.phonecardshop.net.

• An old photograph album will make an ideal storage system for a phone card collection.

LOT 82: CROCODILE AND SNAKESKIN

Recent international regulations governing the use of animal skins means that brand new alligator, crocodile and snakeskin handbags, purses, wallets and travel goods are becoming increasingly rare, and are now out of most people's financial reach.

Items made from these materials are still coveted, however, and thus the older (and more affordable) examples are an excellent subject for a collection. In my opinion, items dating from the 1900s to '40s currently present the best chance for bagging a bargain. Look out in particular for handbags from the 1920s to '40s, as these were excellently made.

The quality of any particular item is all down to the condition of the skin, so be sure to scrutinise this carefully. The finest alligator or crocodile skin pieces are made from the skin on the underbelly of the animal, which has a very distinctive symmetrical pattern. Familiarise yourself with this pattern and you'll be able to identify the highest-quality items.

Items to look out for

• Small alligator, crocodile or snakeskin wallets. Expect to pay £20–£50.
• Alligator, crocodile or snakeskin suitcases. Expect to pay £400–£600.
• Ladies' handbags. These often turn up in charity shops, where they can sometimes be had for as little as £15–£30. Specialist retailers can charge up to £120.
• Vanity mirrors or picture frames are affordable decorative items at £25–£50.
• Crocodile cigar or cigarette cases. Expect to pay £10–£100 depending on size and quality.

TOP TIPS

• Always check for evidence of restoration, and remember that the interior of any item is as important as the exterior.
• Keep your animal-skin items clean. To do so, first remove all the dust and dirt with a damp soft cloth, then stuff the item with tissue paper until it is in its original shape. Next, rub in furniture polish with a very soft cloth (never a brush). Continue rubbing until the item looks as if it were new.
• If the skin is very dry, do not use oils or shoe creams, as this will cause the scales to peel off. Instead, gradually hydrate the skin using a thin coat of solid shoe polish (one which matches the skin colour or is neutral), and rub in with a soft cloth. Wait for the polish to dry, then buff the skin.

LOT 83: TY BEANIE BABIES

The brainchild of US entrepreneur Ty Warner, Beanie Babies became a worldwide phenomenon in the mid- to late-1990s. Though intended as children's toys, they were equally popular with adults as gift items, much like the Cabbage Patch Doll phenomenon of the 1980s.

The official Beanie Babies were mostly made in the shapes of animals, and were usually brightly coloured. Each Baby came with his or her name, birth date and a few lines of poetry. This information was contained on the red heart-shaped tag that was usually affixed to the Baby's ear, and which displayed the 'TY' logo. Most popular amongst the hundreds of different models were the Teddy Bear Beanies, but those with a penchant for the unusual could get hold of an aardvark, coypu or chameleon.

There are two types of Beanie Babies tags: the swing tag (also called the heart tag) and the tush tag. Both types have gone through many changes, and are now known as 'generations'. There are currently 14 generations of swing tags and 13 generations of tush tags! Familiarise yourself with the generations and you will find it easier to secure a bargain.

The rarer Beanie Babies, such as Peanut the Elephant (royal blue) or Humphrey the Camel, might be out of many people's price range. I would suggest, therefore, that you concentrate on Beanie *Buddies* instead. Based on the most popular Babies, this more affordable range was produced in 1998. The Buddies are about 40 percent larger than the Babies, and have a unique soft fabric design.

Items to look out for
• The first nine Beanie Buddies to be produced: Beak the Kiwi Bird, Humphrey the Camel, Jake the Mallard Duck, Peanut the Elephant, Quackers the Duck, Rover the Dog, Stretch the Ostrich, Teddy the Cranberry Bear and Twigs the Giraffe. If the relative rarity is unknown by the seller, you could pick one up for £3–£10, whereas a collector would charge up to £100 per item.

TOP TIPS
• The tag on a Beanie Baby must be intact; without it, the value of the Baby will drop by more than 50 percent.
• Look for Beanies with heart-shaped hard plastic covers that protect their tags.

LOT 84: SWATCH WATCHES

The Swatch watch was launched in 1983 – a water-resistant, shock-proof and brightly coloured watch originally designed to be an inexpensive and throwaway item. For collectors, however, Swatches weren't seen as throwaway at all; with two new styles released per year, and with unique designs and fantastic colours, they were collectable from the start.

Swatch watches were a fad for three or four years, when pretty much anyone and everyone had a boxed Swatch watch for sale or in their collector's cabinet. In fact, I remember many years ago being in London's Oxford Street and spotting a queue of at least 500 people eagerly waiting to get their hands on the new Swatch collection. Much of this hype was down to the marketing of the parent company – the Swatch Watch Company Ltd. Based in Switzerland, it is the largest watch manufacturer in the world.

Over 2,000 models of Swatch watch have been designed at the time of publication, so any collector will have a wide range of themes and colours to choose from. If watch-collecting is your thing, I would suggest you join one of the many members' Websites for collectors (try www.worldcollectorsnet.com, eBay and www.watchswatch.co.uk).

Items to look out for

• The very early models and the limited-edition models can be very costly, with prices up to £250.
• Watches with strange face shapes such as an elongated or 's'-shaped face make the watch more collectable at £50–£120.

TOP TIPS

• Many watches can be bought at boot fairs, antique fairs and antique and charity shops for under £10. Start with pre-2000 Swatches and, once you've familiarised yourself with the styles, colours and designs of that period of Swatch history, move on to pre-1990 models.

• Look out for press releases about any new limited-edition models, especially numbered ones, which the company periodically does. These will often be promoted around Christmas time, and represent a good investment when kept in their original packaging, along with any paperwork relating to the watch.

LOT 85: LLADRO 1953-2000

Tipping future collectables is always made easier if the company in question has a history of growth and success. Lladro porcelain, with its consistent high quality and superior designs, fits snuggle into this bracket.

The Lladro company was founded in 1953 as a small family workshop in Almácera, a tiny farming community near the city of Valencia. Three brothers formed the company after having quit their jobs at the local tile factory. Armed with just a small Moorish kiln that they built in the courtyard of their family house, the brothers quickly established themselves with their uniquely styled contemporary porcelain figurines, which they originally sold at their local market. From these humble beginnings, Lladro now employs over 2,000 people.

Possessing a look and style that is loved by many modern day collectors, Lladro porcelain is so popular today that it is sold in over 120 countries throughout the world. Its output is vast, and includes figurines in the shapes of angels, animals and children, as well as large figural groups and centre pieces. Every piece has a charming title to reflect the pose of the figure, and every year new models are created, some of which are limited editions. Today, Lladro is as popular as it has ever been, with a growing army of collectors worldwide.

Items to look out for
• Pre-1990 single figures cost £40–£80, smaller items go for £30–£40.
• Lladro figures from 1990–2006 can be found at boot fairs for a fraction of their retail price. saw one sold recently for £8!
• Angels, young children and female figures are top of the list for many collectors. Expect to pay £60–£100.

TOP TIPS
• The history of Lladro's figures is well documented, and there are many reference books available, making it easy to research the date of your purchase.
• Always check the hands on human-style figures for damage; on animals check the tails and ears.
• Nao is another brand name for Lladro that is used to sell cheaper versions of the company's output. While less costly, the Nao quality is still very good.
• The Ladro catalogue can be viewed online at www.lladro.com.

LOT 86: TEA CUPS AND SAUCERS

Collecting single tea cups and saucers is a good initiation into the world of antiques, and will give any collector a strong grasp of the styles and designs used in pottery and porcelain from the past to the present day.

Tea-drinking became fashionable in the first quarter of the 18th century with the introduction of tea to England from China and India via the East India Company. The first tea cups were more like bowls, but ladies found that they were burning their fingers on the hot sides, so by 1750 a handle affixed to the bowl had become the norm.

Many of the top 18th-century English factories, among them Worcester, Derby, Chelsea and Wedgwood, produced some very sought-after cups and saucers which can cost collectors up to £1,000. Yet there is no need to spend this sort of money on your collection. Instead, start with 19th-century cups and saucers which turn up in many different guises and are far more affordable. Furthermore, tea cups and saucers are a collecting area in which you can afford to be fussy, so you should never buy restored or damaged items.

Items to look out for

• Nineteenth-century cups and saucers. Expect to pay £5–£20 for a single cup and saucer set. There is so much variety out there that you can quickly build up a collection that represents a wide range of different styles.

• Cups and saucers from the period 1910 to 1970. Examples from this period are very approachable in terms of price, with many costing under £10 per set.

• Imitations of tea cups and saucers by top-name designers such as Clarice Cliff and Susie Cooper (see Lots 30 and 97), produced by the many minor factories that copied their styles. These will cost £7–£15 per set.

• In the late 1990s Wedgwood made copies of some of Clarice Cliff's most famous patterns. These have already risen in price, and will continue to do so. They currently cost £15–£30 per set.

TOP TIPS

• When buying cup and saucer sets, always make sure the cup and saucer match perfectly. This can be done by checking the registration number or pattern number on the bottom of each item.

• Check for signs of restoration and damage, both of which will devalue an item.

99

LOT 87: MEASHAM POTTERY BARGE WARE

Barge ware is quickly becoming a new collecting craze. Its naive charm and crude appearance can be likened to early 18th-century Staffordshire figures.

In the mid 19th century, a potter named William Mason, working from an earthenware pottery at Pool Village in South Derbyshire, started producing teapots made from the local, straw coloured clay. He covered them with a dark-brown 'treacle' glaze and decorated them with a variety of moulded, hand-coloured motifs, including flowers and birds. Most of the teapots sported a plaque on one or both sides that was crudely stamped with messages such as 'God Bless Our Home'.

Measham teapots were created in different sizes, usually measured by capacity, the most common sizes being four to seven pints. The lids are adorned with acorn-shaped finials or miniature teapots. While most teapots have a 'treacle' glaze, there are some in lighter shades as well, and a few have light-green and mid-blue glazes; these are now very rare.

Measham also created other barge ware examples besides teapots, including a tobacco jar, a sugar bowl, a cream jug set, a money box, a spittoon, a vase, a coffee pot, a double-spouted teapot, a tankard, a chamber pot, a loving cup and a smoker's companion set.

Items to look out for

• Nineteenth-century teapots. Depending on size, expect to pay anywhere from £300–£500.
• For single jugs and smaller items, expect to pay from £150–£250.
• A kettle on a stand ranges from £250–£500, depending on size.

TOP TIPS

• One of the rarest Measham items is the chamber pot, which has an eye or a lizard depicted on the bottom of the interior and the following inscription around the rim: 'Pick me up and use me well and what I see I will not tell'. Secrets best not shared!

• Original Measham pottery is rare, but it is possible to buy reproduction Measham. On original Measham, the motto is pressed into the surface of the clay and filled in with blue or black; with reproduction Measham, the lettering is painted on the surface of the plaque with black paint.

LOT 88: MICRO MACHINES

Micro Machines, also known simply as 'Micros', is a line of tiny toy play-sets and vehicles made by Galoob (now owned by Hasbro) in the late 1980s and throughout the 1990s. While not as popular as the 'Hot Wheels' brand, these toys are nonetheless very collectable.

Micro Machines are tiny-scale component-style 'playsets' and vehicles; the average length of a model is 37mm (1½ in). Although Micro Machines have not been sold in the US for some time, newer models are available in the UK and Europe.

The different styles of Micro Machines made include cars, trucks, boats, helicopters, motorcycles, tanks, trains and emergency vehicles. Models were also made of various science fiction franchises, including Star Trek and Star Wars, Power Rangers and Babylon 5. A line of NASCAR cars and playsets was also available, as were play-set Micros featuring miniature vehicles and characters that interact with their play-set environments.

When the Galoob company was sold to Hasbro, the line was discontinued, although imitations can still be found in toy stores.

Items to look out for
• Most Micro Machine play-sets are now worth less than their £5 retail price, although some, like the Civil War set, can command over £10. Others, like the Aliens set of three (based on the 1986 film), can be had for £40.
• Star Trek sets and ships. Some of these are currently being sold on eBay for £75–£200.
• Some individual cars, such as the SVO Mustang. Expect to pay £25.

TOP TIPS
• Military vehicles with accurate markings and certain types of Soviet equipment can be quite valuable. Conducting research on military tanks and aircraft will help you know your stuff.
• Rarer collections, such as Star Trek or Star Wars play-sets, are also valuable.

They even immortalised James Bond and Indiana Jones in micro scale.
• While there are no books on Micros at the time of writing, there are a few websites that can help you learn about and identify the different Micro Machines available. One fun and informative site to check out is www.puremicros.com.

LOT 89: JOHN DITCHFIELD GLASS

John Ditchfield's distinctive and original hand-made art glass is definitely a tip for the top. Ditchfield is already famed amongst collectors, and the prices for his work are sure to keep rising.

John Ditchfield is a Master glass-blower based in England. His company, Glasform, formed in 1985, produces glassware, paperweights and vases in striking colours that have become recognisable across the world. His pieces are magical to behold, with unusual forms and a tactile look that sets them apart from pieces made by other 21st-century glassblowers. Many of his designs and styles have a 'Tiffany' feel to them and, unsurprisingly, Ditchfield has named the famous Arts and Crafts Tiffany Glass Company as one of his major influences.

My mate, David Dickinson, is a big fan of Ditchfield glass. While we were filming the UK television show *Bargain Hunt* together he was on a mission to secure a Ditchfield glass mushroom. I'm pleased to say that David and the show helped John Ditchfield and his beautiful glass reach a wider audience.

Items to look out for
• Signed pieces bought direct from Glasform. Expect to pay £85–£140 for the smaller pieces; £150–£300 for larger examples.
• Unique pieces from the earlier years of Glasform. Like any other collectable, the price will rise where there is rarity factor.
• At the lower end of the price spectrum, Ditchfield's apple-shaped paperweight is a good buy at £40–£60. Note that these were not usually signed.
• Ditchfield's glass designs are widely varied. Recent models include the beehive vase, which costs £260; bon-bon dishes at £120 and a range of bowls and vases which costs £150 and up.
• Small paperweights and delicate novelty shapes can be purchased for under £100.
• Pieces that were originally commissioned by specific buyers. These will be rare and pricey.

TOP TIPS
• Only buy from bona fide dealers or direct from the factory at www.glasform.com. This way you will be 100 percent sure that the item is genuine. There are some very convincing copies out there.
• It is possible to visit the Ditchfield studio. Visit the website for more information.

LOT 90: SHERATON REVIVAL FURNITURE

The Edwardian period was short, from 1901 to 1910, yet it produced some superb examples of furniture. Many Edwardian pieces were inspired by earlier cabinet-makers, particularly Thomas Sheraton, and so the period became known as the Sheraton Revival Period.

The Sheraton Revival was a breath of fresh air after the dark and sometimes heavy furniture styles of the Victorian period, and was ideally suited to the elegant homes being built at the time. Almost all Sheraton Revival pieces are delicate to look at, with the use of rich mahogany and satin-wood banding.

This was the age of the craftsman cabinet-maker, and the furniture really does stand the test of time. Many items were aimed at the lady of the house, with exquisite examples of writing desks, dressing tables with heart-shaped mirrors and music-room suites made to look at rather than sit on.

The Sheraton Revival look became so popular that many top cabinet-makers of the day were forced to follow the fashion, with established companies like Waring & Gillows introducing some pieces that could easily have been taken for genuine Sheraton-period furniture.

Items to look out for
• Bedroom suites comprising two wardrobes, bed ends, two bedside cupboards and a dressing table. Expect to pay £350–£500 at auction for a complete suite.
• Edwardian side tables, coffee tables and writing desks. Expect to pay £50–£120 for a side table and £200–£500 for a writing desk, depending on style and size.
• Items by the famous English furniture-makers Waring & Gillows. For example, Waring & Gillows pedestal desks are of superior quality and are still a relatively good value at £1,200–£1,500.
• Small inlaid side tables and coffee tables can be picked up for £150–£250 at auction.

TOP TIPS
• Sheraton Revival furniture can be delicate, so check for signs of damage or repair on the slender tapering legs.
• Elegant, stylish handles are a must on this style of furniture.
• The commonly used satin-wood inlay can lift when exposed to heat or sunlight.

LOT 91: MINIATURE FURNITURE

Originating in the 18th century but more widely available in the 19th and early 20th centuries, these charming miniature pieces were a manufacturer's way of showing prospective furniture buyers a sample of the craftsmanship they could expect if they were to order the manufacturer's items.

Referred to in the antiques trade as 'apprentice pieces' or 'salesman samples', miniature items were, for all intents and purposes, an exact copy of their full-size equivalents, right down to the handles, locks and even the wood grains. Most were finely made by apprentice cabinet-makers under the watchful eye of the master craftsman.

Miniature examples exist for virtually every type of furniture, including chairs, wardrobes, chests of drawers, bureaux, sideboards, beds and clocks, so for a collector the opportunities are endless. Miniature furniture should not, however, be confused with doll's house furniture; an apprentice piece should measure from 15cm–45cm (6 in–18 in) tall.

Items to look out for

• Intricately detailed or very delicate late 18th- and early 19th-century models. These can cost up to £3,000.

• Late 19th- and early 20th-century models. A simple bun-foot chest will cost about £75–£150; more elaborate and delicate pieces can go for over £750.

• Pieces by top retailers such as Asprey, who produced a miniature range in 1910, are popular with collectors because of their superior quality. Expect to pay up to £2,000 per item.

• Early 20th-century models. These are often overlooked by serious collectors because of their style or age, so you can bag a bargain here. Expect to pay £50–£150.

TOP TIPS

• Look after your miniature-furniture collection as you do your life-size furniture: with a good coat of wax two or three times a year to enhance the patina and a gentle dusting every week.

• Never keep your collection too close to a heating system or in direct sunlight, or it may become damaged.

• Try to house your furniture behind glass, as this offers good protection.

• Look at a miniature piece as you would any other piece of furniture: examine it for quality and look for signs of restoration.

LOT 92: COSTUME JEWELLERY 1940–1980

In the age of 'bling', costume jewellery has really found its place again. Today's high-street jewellers, and even some supermarkets and mega-stores, have a good – and better yet, affordable – range of costume jewellery on display.

Over the last 30 years, costume jewellery has become a well-established collectable, but this has mainly been the case with pieces from the 1920s to the '40s. It is therefore, in my opinion, worth taking a closer look at jewellery from the 1940s to the '80s.

Many US costume jewellery makers are still in business today, and it is worth parting with that little bit extra for the bonus of a named product. Notable American designers include Napier, Trifari, Joseff of Hollywood and Miriam Haskell. Scandinavia also produced a good range of costume jewellery during his period, with many pieces in silver. (Look out for the number 800, the marking for silver on the Continent, on the inside of the piece.) Notable designers include Georg Jensen and Swarovski.

Items to look out for

• For single costume jewellery items, expect to pay between £5 and £10, depending on the size and quality.
• Job lots at an auction sale are priced in accordance with the number of items in the lot. Allow £1.50–£2.50 per item.
• Pieces by well-known designers such as Christian Dior, Kenneth J. Lane and Coco Chanel will not be cheap, but they will certainly be of superior quality. Expect to pay £80–£150 per item, depending on the age, intricacy and size of the piece.

TOP TIPS

• Look for a style of jewellery that appeals to you and concentrate on finding pieces in this style. For example, many people collect insect shapes such as butterflies and bees because they are timeless.
• Quality is important. Make sure you are armed with a good spyglass and check that the setting is in good order and that no stones or pieces of glass are missing.
• Boot fairs and garage sales are good hunting grounds. You should expect to pay a fraction of the price you would in high-street shops or at antiques fairs.

LOT 93: AVON SCENT BOTTLES

In 1880 a young American businessman called David H. McConnell started selling books door to door. In order to entice more customers, he decided to give away a complimentary bottle of cologne with every book purchase. It wasn't long before he realised that the perfume was more popular than the books, and by 1939 the company had metamorphosed into Avon Products.

Who can forget the company's famous catch-phrase, 'Avon Calling!', which was used extensively in its advertising campaigns from the 1950s to the '80s; or the Avon agent, normally a well-dressed lady who would leave you a catalogue to browse through and make your selections, then call back the following week to collect the catalogue and the all-important order.

The Avon catalogue offered a considerable range of perfumes, with the colognes being the most popular. The perfume was cheap and cheerful but the novelty factor was the unusually shaped bottles, and this is what I believe will become a strong collecting area in the coming years.

Different novelty bottles were introduced almost weekly, so there is a huge variety to choose from, including those in the shapes of dogs, cats, ballerinas, Wellington boots, ships and teapots. Avon made after-shave for men and scents and soap for children, too, and these bottles are collectable as well. Many people have kept their old bottles, so what was once a throwaway item is now a burgeoning collector's field.

Items to look out for
• Unused bottles in their original packaging. Expect to pay £10–£20.
• Bottles with unused perfume but no packaging. Expect to pay £2–£10, depending on the shape of the bottle.
• Bottles which have been used are still collectable; these can be picked up at boot fairs and charity shops for between 50p and £2.

TOP TIPS
• There are actually books out there on collecting Avon bottles. These can be invaluable sources of information.

• There are also websites geared specifically for Avon bottle collectors. One particularly informative website is www.findavon.com.

LOT 94: ART DECO WALL MIRRORS

The Art Deco period was a time of style and elegance, and Art Deco pieces are as fashionable in the home today as they were in the 1930s. Wall mirrors seem to epitomise the angular, geometric look that so many people look for when buying Art Deco. They are also relatively affordable and eminently useful.

Bedroom mirrors were very popular in the 1930s, and some of the samples from this period will have engraved or etched decoration. (Usually this decoration is comprised of a single section, but I have also seen some with several sections.) Vanity mirrors or shaving mirrors, though small, retain the style of the larger examples, and have all the charm of the Art Deco period.

Keep your eyes open for mirrors with multiple glass sections. These come in sunburst shapes of all sizes, and most have clear and coloured glass sections running through them. Other shapes to look out for include the rectangular and round designs; these were made in prolific numbers and are readily avail-able. The peacock-tail design – a large wall mirror in the form of a peacock's tail and similar to a hand fan – is equally collectable. Other, rarer designs include mirrors in the shapes of musical instruments, fish or boats; these will be harder to find and, accordingly, more valuable.

Items to look out for
• Plain or etched small bathroom or vanity mirrors. Expect to pay £25–£50; £50–£100 for clear and coloured sectional examples.
• Medium-to-large wall mirrors. Expect to pay £75–£150, depending on colour.
• The most unusual shapes can cost up to £750. These really are works of art.

TOP TIPS
• Make sure that the mirror's glass is original by checking the colour of each section. You will usually notice a different shade in any replacement glass.
• Look for a strong Art Deco feel when buying, as this will enhance the item's value.
• The 1950s and '60s saw an Art Deco revival, and many mirrors were produced in the style during that time. The only way you can tell the difference between these and the original '30s mirrors is by doing your research. Get the view of an expert if in doubt.

LOT 95: GERLINOL TEA TROLLEY

If you are a regular viewer of the UK television show *Bargain Hunt*, you will know about the Gerlinol tea trolley. Every time I see one for sale I try to guide my team towards buying it, and each time they have done so they have made a profit!

This collapsible trolley is German-made, and originates from around 1955. The Gerlinol has laminate wood shelves which fold up with a spring mechanism and a chrome-plated steel tubular frame on wheels. Rosewood laminate is the most common material for the shelves, but there are also examples in simulated mahogany or oak. Sometimes the wood is colour-stained. This versatile trolly can serve as a double display shelf for CDs or books when folded up, and when opened out it can be used to hold glassware and, of course, tea paraphenalia.

The Gerlinol's strong, stylised look makes it appear more contemporary than it actually is. Little is known about the designer or the factory, but don't let that put you off buying

one; as they become more collectable – which I firmly believe they will – more information will come to light. Compared with the many styles of Art Deco chrome tea trolleys available, which could set you back anything from £150 to £500, the Gerlinol is a snip. For a fraction of the price you'll have a multifunctional item that will one day become an icon of 1950s style.

Items to look out for
• The rosewood-laminate tea trolley. Expect to pay £75–£100 from a dealer, although they sometimes show up at auction for as little as £40.
• Examples with colour-stained woods will set you back about £100–£125.

TOP TIPS
• Be quick off the mark and you could find a real bargain. A trawl though internet auction sites show Gerlinols being sold at incredibly low prices. The last one I bought cost £15 plus postage (most examples are still to be found on the Continent).

• Make sure the spring action is functioning correctly, and also ensure that the chrome legs show no signs of corrosion or rust.
• You can check for authenticity by looking on the underside of the trolley for the Gerlinol factory stamp or mark.

LOT 96: WATERING CANS

I have been amazed at the price increase of watering cans and other garden-related items. Two years ago it was rare to see watering cans for sale at antique fairs, yet today you will see them there being sold for £25 to £65. The reason for this increase in popularity is that so many people now use their gardens as living areas, and want to decorate their surroundings in an authentic way.

From the late 19th century until the 1940s, it was fashionable for manufacturers to produce specialist watering cans. Typically small, these were usually hand-crafted and intended for watering household plants. Many had an ornamental theme; some were even made in the forms of animals, while others were made with extra-long spouts. The vast majority of cans were made from galvanised steel or alloy, and the more costly ones had an enamel finish.

Items to look out for

• Late 19th- and early 20th-century cans in good condition are quite rare. Small decorative cans from this period can be worth anywhere from £25–£75.
• Standard-size models in a plain design are worth £15–£25; enamel-finished and coloured cans are worth £40–£60.
• Watering cans made from 1930 through to 1970 were made in the traditional way, but feel lighter to hold. These can be worth £15–£30.
• Brass and copper was a popular material combination for cans made in Edwardian times. Such examples are worth £30–£75.
• Enamel watering cans were made in various colours, including green, yellow, white and blue. These are worth £20–£40.
• Hand-painted and crested cans, or examples with advertising logos, are the top-end pieces for collections. These cost £75–£200.
• Shell, Esso and Castor Oil produced watering cans in the 1950s solely for the use of topping up radiators or cleaning window screens. Coveted by collectors, these cost £75–£120.

TOP TIPS
• Make sure that the can still works, and that it has no holes or perforations.
• Check thoroughly for signs of repair or corrosion; both will devalue a can.
• If the can feels light when you pick it up, it likely dates anywhere from the 1930s through to the 1970s.

LOT 97: SUSIE COOPER

Susie Cooper's name is synonymous with excellent ceramic design. Like Clarice Cliff, she was one of the most important and prolific British designers of her time.

Born in 1902 in Burslem, Stoke on Trent, Susie first studied at the Burslem School of Art. She went on to join the A.E. Gray pottery, where she eventually became resident designer.

It was her work at the A.E. Gray pottery through the 1920s which stamped Susie Cooper's designed authority. It was then that she produced her fantastic lustre ware and geometric patterns, and Gray's launched a factory mark in her honour: a steamship at full speed that incorporated the words 'Designed by Susie Cooper'.

In 1929, Susie decided to strike out on her own, and established the Susie Cooper Pottery. After a series of relocations, in 1931 she moved into her famous studio, 'Crown Works'. It was then that she introduced the famous 'Cube Shape' range, still one of her most collectable. Another highly collectable design, the 'Kestrel' range, was also begun

around this time. (Kestrel is one of the longest lived designs of Susie Cooper, and spanned from 1932–1950.)

In 1966, facing financial difficulties, Susie Cooper Productions, as her company was now called, was taken over by the Wedgwood Group. She worked with Wedgwood through the 1960s and '70s, producing such popular patterns as 'Carnaby Daisy' and 'Cornpoppy'. She worked with Wedgwood until 1986, when she moved to the Isle of Man and worked as a freelance designer until her death in 1995.

Items to look out for

• Early works from the period 1920–30 take prime position in many collections. The Cubist and geometric designs and patterns will set you back £300–£3000.
• Banded ware from the 1930s–50s. The Kestrel design is worth £30–£50.

110

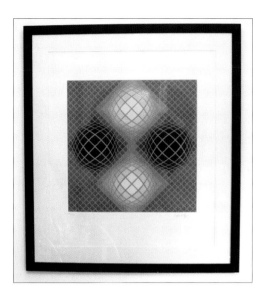

LOT 98: VICTOR VASARELY

A Hungarian artist and architect who passed away in 1997, Victor Vasarely is now considered by many connoisseurs of modern art to be the leading artist in 'Op art'. Although not to everyone's taste, his vibrantly coloured silk screen prints are both stunning and highly collectable.

Born in 1906 in Hungary, Vasarely studied applied graphic art and typographic design in Budapest. He left Hungary for Paris in 1930, where he worked as a graphic artist and creative consultant for an advertising agency. In 1938 he created what is considered the first true piece of 'Op art'; entitled *Zebras*, the work consisted of curved black-and-white stripes.

Over the next three decades Vasarely developed his unique style of geometric abstract art, working with various materials, including silk screen, and experimenting with textural effects, perspective, shadow and light. Through the 1950s he defined the visual elements of what eventually became known as 'Op art', and was designated the father of the movement. After a prolific careeer that resulted in numerous awards, including the International Guggenheim Award in New York (1964), Vasarely died in 1997.

If you like the psychedelic aesthetic of the 1960s and '70s, then Vasarely is a good artist to collect. Many of his silk screen prints are held in high esteem by modern art collectors, and his work has a cult following, but at the time of writing prices for his work have remained unchanged for the past 15 years.

Items to look out for
• Vasarely prints from the 1960s and '70s cost £800–£1200 if buying from galleries or specialists dealers, but they can be snapped up for much less at auction (see Top Tips below).

TOP TIPS
• Victor Vaserly's work can sometimes be bought cheaply at auction. I recently bought a piece for a mere £65 that I'm sure was worth over £400.
• If buying a print, bear in mind that the lower the edition number, the more valuable the piece.
• Always try to buy an artist's-proof print. Most sought after by collectors, these are prints that were hand-signed by the artist for quality control and colour correctness.

LOT 99: LORNA BAILEY

I have no doubt that Lorna Bailey's designs are highly collectable as 'future antiques'. Thought by many to be the next Clarice Cliff, her hand-painted ceramic designs are so popular that they have spawned a collectors' club that currently boasts over 1,000 members.

Born in 1978 in Newcastle-under-Thyme, Staffordshire, Lorna began collecting Clarice Cliff and Susie Cooper designs as a child. She went on to attend Stoke-on-Trent College, where she studied design. While she was still a student, a major pottery factory, Woods & Sons, went into liquidation, and its assets were being sold. Luckily for Lorna, her father and a friend together purchased some of Woods & Sons' assets and took over a near-by pottery, where they began producing hand-painted wares.

Lorna spent all of her free time painting traditional wares for the business, as well as experimenting with her own designs. Slowly sales of Lorna's work increased, and by 1998 Lorna and two members of staff were hand-painting her designs exclusively. Her pieces, which have a stylised Art Deco feel to them, are currently selling almost as fast as she makes them, and I believe their value can only continue to rise.

Items to look out for

• The Astro sugar sifter. Commissioned in 1998 by *Collect It* antiques magazine, Lorna created a limited edition of 250 sifters. The whole edition sold out immediately. If you can find a sifter, it will likely go for around £100.
• Early pieces, such as uniquely shaped vases, can cost up to £400.
• Lorna has just produced some limited-edition figurines, including a series depicting The Beatles. These figurines now cost £30–£100, and their value is sure to rise.
• Fridge magnets, currently a bargain at £6.

TOP TIPS
• All limited edition Lorna Bailey items will be numbered on the base.
• The more unusual the shape, whether a figurine or a vase, the more collectable the item will be.
• You can join the Lorna Bailey members club and receive special deals and editions that are only offered to its members. Check out www.lorna-bailey.co.uk.

LOT 100: CHARLES AND RAY EAMES

Husband and wife team Charles and Ray Eames was one of the most dynamic and multi-talented design partnerships of the 20th century. Described by their friends as humanitarians, they wanted above all that their designs should be enjoyed as part of an 'open, organic and emotionally expressive lifestyle'.

Born in 1907 in Saint Louis, Missouri, Charles Eames briefly studied architecture, but was dismissed from school when he refused to cease his interest in modern architects. He went on to study at the Cranbrook Academy of Art in Michigan, where he became head of the industrial design department. He married his colleague, Ray Kaiser, in 1941, and they moved to Los Angeles, California.

By 1942 Ray Eames was already experimenting with plywood, and had produced two organic plywood sculptured chairs, illustrating her interest in the avant-garde movement.

The Eames's first major joint project was their own house, which they named Eames House, Case Study House #8. The house was a perfect example of an economical space for both living and working, reflecting the modernist ideas espoused by the Bauhaus group.

In the 1950s the Eameses began designing furniture, producing such classics as the Eames Lounge Chair and Ottoman (designed in 1956 as a birthday gift for friend Billy Wilder, the film director), the Aluminum Group Furniture (1958) and the Eames Chaise (1968).

Items to look out for
• The Eames Lounge Chair and Ottoman. A set will cost £1,500-£3,000 at auction and around £4,000 retail.
• The moulded fiberglass seat on an Eiffel-tower-shaped wire base known as the Eiffel Chair. These cost £150 per chair at auction; £300–£400 retail.
• Smaller items like the Eames Children's Chair costs around £250 retail.
• Plywood-and-steel storage units; these cost around £700 retail.

TOP TIP
• The year 2006 marks the 50th anniversary of the Eames Lounge Chair and Ottoman. In celebration, all chairs manufactured in 2006 will feature a medallion affixed to the bottom. These will no doubt be very collectable, and their value is sure to rise in the future.

LOT 101: WHITEFRIARS GLASS 1960-1980

Whitefriars glass will no doubt have a permanent place in collecting history. Prices have increased dramatically in the last few years, but prices are now falling for certain models, particularly those from the 1970s, making them a great bargain.

The small glassworks that would come to be known as Whitefriars originated in 1720 in a small space off Fleet Street, in London. In 1834 the glassworks was purchased by James Powell, a London wine mechant and entrepeneur; thereafter it became known as James Powell & Sons. The company began to produce stained-glass windows, becoming leaders in the field when hundreds of new Victorian churches were being built across the country. By the late 1850s the firm had begun to design and produce the domestic table glass for which it is best known today.

In 1926 the company moved to Wealdstone, near Harrow, and became known as Powell & Sons (Whitefriars) Ltd. Designer Geoffrey Baxter joined the company in 1954, and designed the popular 'Textured' range in 1967. Initially available in three colours – cin-

namon, indigo and willow – with blue and tangerine introduced two years later, the range was an immediate hit. Also released around this time were the Studio Ranges, designed by artists such as Peter Wheeler. Whitefriars continued to make textured domestic glass through the 1970s, notably the 1972 Glacier range, but sadly, the factory closed in 1980.

Items to look out for

• Geoffrey Baxter's Drunken Bricklayer vase. A small example will cost £250, a medium one £400 and a large one over £600. The Banjo vase will cost around £600 and the TV vase around £250.

• 1970s textured vases, unless rare, will usually cost £50–£80, depending on colour and size. Larger items from this period can cost over £200.

TOP TIPS

• Textured Whitefriars glass from the 1970s is often cheaper than 1960s examples, but it is not as collectable – or at least

not at the moment!

• Not all Whitefriars glass is marked, so avoid fakes by familiarising yourself with the real thing.

GLOSSARIES

Auction Room Glossary

Absentee bid: Leaving a bid with the auction house so that it can bid on your behalf.

Auctioneer: The person sitting on the rostrum wielding the gavel and monitoring the bids.

Auction fever: The situation that occurs when a bidder forgets the true value of a lot and bids like a headless chicken.

Auction preview: The days that are allocated for prospective buyers to view all of the items and lots in the saleroom.

Bidders: The people in the saleroom who are attempting to buy goods.

Bidding off the wall: A term used for an auctioneer who is taking bids from the wall to get up to a reserve price.

Buyer's premium: The sum that is added to the hammer price and paid to the auction house. It ranges from 5–25 percent of the final bid and VAT is usually added.

Cashier: The person who has the pleasure of taking your money when you have bid successfully on a lot.

Catalogue: The publication available from the auctioneer on viewing days and sale days. It contains a complete list of all items entered into the auction.

Commission bid: A bid that is written on a form supplied by the auction house so that they can execute the bid for you.

Condition report: A detailed description of the state of a lot. It can be obtained from the auctioneers via email, phone, post or in person.

Dealers: These are the professionals that you often see huddled together in an auction room – this breed of bidder can be quite disruptive.

Defaulting on a bid: When you do not fulfil a bid. This can be very costly, as the auction house can pursue a claim against you if you do not pay for and collect the lot you bid on in the auction.

Estimates: These figures are provided as a guide to prospective buyers, and are normally based around a reserve price (see below).

Hammer price: The final price you pay when the auctioneer's hammer drops.

Invoice: This will list each lot you have purchased, how much you paid for each lot and the total amount you have spent, with the buyer's premium and VAT added.

Lot number: The number given to each item coming up for auction.

Paddle number: The specific number that is allocated to each buyer after registration (see below).

Porters: These are the happy faces that walk around the saleroom and point out the lots as they are coming under the hammer. They will also help you pack and move your goods at the end of the sale.

Registering to bid: This is normally done in the head cashier's office. You register with your name, address and some form of identification. Once this is completed you will be given a paddle number with which to bid in the auction.

Reserve Price: A price agreed between the auction room and yourself if you are the vendor.

Selling rate: The number of lots the auctioneer normally sells per hour. This is usually between 80 and 300 lots.

Storage charges: The charge you have to pay if you are late in clearing your items from the saleroom.

Telephone bid: A pre-arranged telephone link that is booked with the auctioneer for the lots you would like to bid on. This method allows bidders to remain anonymous.

Terms of business: The legal jargon that is normally displayed at the back of the saleroom or in the catalogue.

Terms of payment: Most auction houses accept cheques, cash and all major credit cards.

Valuations: The price given to an item by the head valuer of the saleroom.

Vendor: A technical term for a seller of goods at an auction house.

Withdrawn lots: Items taken out of a sale by an auction house.

Clock Glossary

Automation: Figures that move or strike on the hour and the quarter-hour.

Balance wheel: The mechanism that controls the movement of a watch or a clock.

Bezel: The ring that secures the glass cover to the dial on a watch or a clock.

Calendar aperture: The small window on some dials that displays the day of the month, and sometimes the month as well.

Chapter ring: The part of the dial on which the hour numbers are painted, engraved or attached.

Escapement: The part of the clock that regulates it and provides the impulse to the chain, pendulum or balance.

Hood: The part of a long-case clock that lifts off the top to provide access to the movement.

Pendulum: The device that swings at a fixed rate and controls the timekeeping.

Repeat button: A small device that lets the clock repeat the last hour or quarter of an hour when a cord is pulled or a button is pressed.

Furniture Glossary

Apron: The decorative shaped skirt of wood that runs under the drawers and between the legs of a table or feet of a chest.

Ballester: The shaped turning or slender pillar with a bullbats base that is used on the legs and pedestals of some tables.

Banding: Decorative veneers used around the edges of some tables, drawers and other items of furniture.

Barley twist: A spiral shape normally favoured for turned legs during the second half of the 19th century. The pattern is still in use today.

Bergère: A French term that is applied to chairs with caned backs and seats.

Boulle work: A form of marquetry using brass and tortoiseshell that was very popular in the 19th century.

Bow front: An outwardly curved front that is found mainly on a chest of drawers, or sideboards.

Break front: A term normally used for a piece of furniture with a protruding centre section.

Brush-in slide: The pull-out slide found on the top of a chest of drawers, normally associated with 18th-century bachelor's chests.

Bun foot: A flattened version of a ball foot that was very popular in Victorian times.

Bureau: A writing desk with a tall front that normally encloses a fitted interior; many also have drawers below.

Cabriole leg: A curving S-shaped leg used on tables and chairs that is synonymous with the 18th century.

Canterbury: A small container used for sheet music or papers.

Chesterfield: A deep-buttoned upholstered settee with no wood showing.

Cheval mirror: A tall, freestanding dressing mirror that is supported by two uprights.

Chinoiserie: Oriental-style decoration or a lacquered pattern applied to furniture.

Claw and ball foot: A support modelled as a ball gripped by a claw.

Commode: A highly decorated chest of drawers or cabinet that is also called 'bombe shaped'.

Console table: A table that stands against a wall, normally between windows. They sometimes have matching mirrors above and can come in pairs.

Corner chair: A chair with backed splats on two sides that is intended to stand in the corner of a room.

Davenport: A small, compact writing unit that normally has a flight of drawers and a sloped top for writing.

Drop-in seat: An upholstered seat frame that sits in the main framework of a chair.

Drop leaf: A table with a fixed central section and hinged sides.

Figuring: The natural grain of wood seen in veneer.

Finial: A decorative turned knob normally applied to the top of bookcases and bureaus.

Frieze: The framework immediately below a tabletop.

Harlequin: A term used to describe a set of

chairs that are similar but do not match.

Inlay: Normally brass, mother of pearl or veneer, these are set into the surface of a solid piece of furniture or wood.

Ladderback: A chair with a series of horizontal back rails.

Lion's paw feet: A foot carved as a lion's paw, this style was very popular in the 18th century, but also found on brass castors from the early 19th century.

Loo table: A large table that is normally circular.

Marquetry: A highly decorative form of inlay using numerous veneers.

Ormolu: A mount or article that is gilded or gold coloured.

Over-mantle mirror: A mirror designed to hang over a mantlepiece.

Papier mâché: Pulped paper that is moulded to make small trays or small items of furniture.

Parquetry: A geometrical pattern made from small pieces of veneer.

Patina: The build up of wax and dirt that gives old furniture its unique look.

Pedestal desk: A flat desk, usually with a leather top, that stands on two flights of drawers.

Pembroke table: A small side table with two small flaps.

Pie-crust top: The carved or moulded decoration to the edge of a table.

Pole screen: An adjustable fire screen.

Runners: The strips of wood on which drawers slide in and out.

Side table: Any table designed to stand against the wall.

Sofa table: Normally a rectangular table with two small, hinged flaps at the ends. Designed to stand directly behind a sofa.

Stretchers: The horizontal bars that strengthen chairs.

Stuff-over seat: A chair that is upholstered over the seat rails.

Teapoy: A small 19th century piece of furniture designed for holding tea leaves.

Toilet mirror: A small dressing mirror with a drawer below.

Trefoil: Any item that resembles a clover leaf.

Wot not: A stand with open shelves of the type popular in the 19th century.

Wheel-backed chair: A chair with a circular back and spoke-like support.

Pottery and porcelain Glossary

Applied decoration: Anything that is attached to a piece rather than being a part of the main body.

Baluster vase: A vase with a curved shape and a narrow stem or neck.

Basalt: A black volcanic stoneware, used frequently by Wedgwood.

Blue and white: A general term used for porcelain and earthenware that normally has a Chinese decoration.

Blanc de Chine: A very translucent type of Chinese porcelain that is still being produced today. It is left unpainted and has a thick glaze.

Bone china: A term commonly used for English porcelain.

Cabinet ware: Plates, cups and saucers made for display rather than for everyday use. These pieces are normally hand-painted and of good quality.

Cancellation mark: One or two strokes through the factory mark that let the buyer know that the item is flawed and not of their normal standard.

Cartouche: A decorative oval frame that is set within the porcelain and normally hand-painted or printed.

Celadon: A term used for the green glaze that is often used on Chinese stoneware.

Chocolate cup: A large cup with two handles, a cover and a matching saucer.

Coffee can: A straight-sided cylindrical cup with no handles in a style made famous by Sèvres.

Commemorative ware: Any item that commemorates an event, such as a wedding, jubilee or battle.

Crackleware: A form of decoration used on an item, normally Chinese.

Crazing: Tiny surface cracks in the glaze of a piece of porcelain that has been caused by technical defects.

Delft ware: Earthenware made in the Netherlands with a tin glaze (see opposite).

Enamels: The bright colours applied to pottery and porcelain as over-glazed decoration (see below).

Faïence ware: Tin-glazed earthenware that is normally made in France, Germany and other Continental countries.

Famille rose or verte: Chinese decoration of either pink (rose) or green (verte) enamel.

Firing crack: Damage to a piece of pottery that has occurred during firing.

Flambé: A bright crimson glaze.

Flat back: A term used for a Staffordshire figure that has a plain, flat back so that it stands easily on a mantlepiece or fireplace.

Gilding: A term used for the application of gold, normally to the banding of porcelain made in the Chinese manner.

Impressed mark: A mark that is indented into the piece by the factory makers.

Incised mark: A mark that is scratched into the surface.

Ironstone china: A type of English stoneware made famous by Masons.

Jardinière: A plant or flower container, these are sometimes formed of two pieces with a matching stand.

Lead-glazed: A type of transparent glaze that incorporated lead oxide.

Loving cup: A twin-handled cup that is normally urn shaped. This style was made by many potteries.

Moustache cup: A cup that is specially designed so that its lower lip protects the user from being left with a soiled moustache.

Over-glazed: This is decoration painted or printed to the piece of pottery or porcelain after glazing.

Parian ware: Un-glazed biscuit porcelain similar to Parian marble. It was very popular in 19th century England and the United States for figures and figurines.

Pearl ware: A very durable form of white porcelain that was particularly popular at Wedgwood.

Porcelain: A translucent white ceramic that is very fragile.

Pottery: A generic term for all ceramics, excluding porcelain.

Puzzle jug: An unusual jug with a globular body and three or seven spouts at the rim.

Rococo: A popular style of mid-18th century decoration, which is normally asymmetric and with the use of scrolls.

Soft-paste porcelain: Another term for porcelain which is made in a particular way.

Staffordshire: A generic term for English pottery made in the Midlands.

Studio pottery: Pottery that has been individually designed and crafted.

Tea bowl: A small cup inspired by the Oriental fashion for tea. These bowls have no handles and were mass-produced.

Terracotta: Lightly fired red earthenware that is not usually glazed.

Tin glaze: An opaque white glaze containing tin, popular in the 18th and 19th centuries and often used on majolica and toby jugs.

Transfer print: A form of decoration which uses a printed engraving.

Silver glossary

Assay mark: A date-stamp given to silver produced in Britain, Ireland and Scotland that indicates that the silver has been properly tested and is pure.

Beading: A decorative border of small beads around an item of silver.

Bezel: The inner rim of a cover, it is normally in descriptions of coffee pots and teapots.

Britannia standard: A rare mark used on British silver between 1690–1720 which indicates goods of a high quality.

British plate: An early version of silver-plating which dates from the 1830s–1850s, and was thereafter called electroplating (see over).

Canteen: A box used to contain cutlery; it normally houses a full service for 8-12 people.

Cartouche: A decorative frame or panel that normally surrounds a coat of arms.

Castor: A two-piece item that is used for sprinkling salt, pepper and sugar.

Chalice: Another name for a goblet or wine cup of the type often used at Catholic or Church of England services.

Charger: A large dish or plate which is

normally circular or oval in shape.

Chasing: Decoration that is worked into a silver item with a hammer or a punch. This sort of pattern is raised above the surface.

Cruet: The framework for castors and bottles containing condiments, such as salt, pepper, oil or vinegar.

Dish ring: An unusual item of silver normally used to keep hotplates away from the table surface. These pieces usually have concave sides, pierced work and come in animal shapes. They are similar to an item of silver called a 'potato ring', and almost exclusively Irish.

Electroplating: Also know as E.P.N.S or E.P. on copper, this is silver applied over a copper of nickel alloy, and is a style that was in use from about 1840.

Ewer: A large jug with a lip that is often part of a set with a basin. It is sometimes used to contain water so that diners can wash their hands during meals.

Filigree: Open decorative panels with small silver beads. Today's filigree normally comes from Spain, India or Africa.

Flatware: Technically this is a term for all flat objects such as plates and silver, but more recently it has been applied to services of spoons and forks.

Floating or erasure: To remove an existing coat of arms and replace it with another.

Gardroning: A border around the edge of an item, usually formed from a succession of loaves and flutes.

Gilding: A method of applying a gold finish to silver or electroplated items.

Right cut: A common form of engraving that makes the design work stand out more sharply.

Salver: A flat dish which is similar to a serving tray, but has no handles.

Sheffield plate: A silver substitute that was used in the early 18th century. The plate was made by binding and fusing sterling silver and copper.

Sterling silver: An English term for silver that contains at least 9.25 percent pure silver.

RECOMMENDED BUYING AND SELLING VENUES

Alfies Antique Market
13-25 Church Street
London NW8 8DT
020 7723 6066
www.alfiesantiques.com
Large indoor market with dealers selling wares from the 18th to the 20th century.

Bagham Barn Antiques
Canterbury Road
Chilham
Kent CT4 8DU
01227 732522
www.baghambarn.com

Camden Passage Market
Camden Passage
London N1
www.camdenpassageislington.co.uk
The selection here runs the gamut from Art Deco and Victorian treasures to watercolours and modern furniture. Held every Wednesday and Saturday.

Cameo Auctions
Kennet Holme Farm
Bath Road
Midgham
Berkshire RG7 5UX
01189 713772
www.cameo-auctioneers.co.uk

Dreweatt Neate
Tunbridge Wells Salerooms
The Auction Halls
Linden Park Road
The Pantiles
Tunbridge Wells
Kent TN2 5QL
www.dnfa.com/tunbridgewells
01635 553553
Buying and selling online.

David Lay
The Penzance Auction House
Alverton
Penzance
Cornwall TR18 4RE
01736 361414
www.invaluable.com/partnerpages

Horners the Auctioneers
Old Norwich Road
Acle
Norfolk NR13 3BY
0800 9754416
www.horners.co.uk

Philip Serrel
The Malvern Saleroom
Barnards Green Road
Malvern
Worcestershire WR14 3LW
01684 892314
www.serrell.com

Portobello Market
Portobello Road,
London W11
www.portobelloroad.co.uk
World-famous market selling antiques of all kinds, jewellery, second-hand clothes and bric-a-brac. Some dealers are open during the week, but most open only on Saturdays.

Shapes Auctioneers & Valuers
Bankhead Avenue
Sighthill
Edinburgh EH11 4BY
0131 4533222
www.shapesauctioneers.co.uk

Websites

www antiquestradegazette.com
Online catalogue and list of forthcoming live auctions.

www.invaluble.com
Providers of auction dates, online sales catalogues and price guides. Catalogue search engine that can search for specific items.

www.antiques-atlas.com
Lists most antiques fairs in the UK, often well in advance.

www.sothebys.com
Online catalogue, plus auction results and calendar of upcoming events.

During the 1940s, London retailer Heal's represented some of the top designers of the day, including Lucy Rie, Roger Nicholson, Keith Murray and Lucienne Day. Furniture from this period is very collectable.

West German vases from the 1970s, with their volcanic look and dripping, vibrant colours or spider's web patterns, are highly sought after, particularly when found as an intact set.

ENGLAND

- 1890–1924 Arts and Crafts and Art Nouveau

- 1920–1940 Art Deco

- 1951 Festival of Britain Exhibition

- 1940–1960 Utility Movement

- 1970 Pop Art

- Late 1970s–1980s Punk Rock

- 1980–2000 Post Modernism

GERMANY

- 1900–1924 Arts and Crafts and Art Nouveau

- 1910–1925 Bauhaus Movement

- 1924–1940 Functionalism (tubular metal furniture)

Danish Holmegaard glass from 1940-1970 has become very collectable in the past few years, particularly those ranges designed by in-house designers Per Lütken and Michael Bang.

Modernist designs, such as this molded plastic table and chair in the style of Charles and Ray Eames, are highly sought after, and buyers are now paying a premium for this aesthetic.

SCANDINAVIA

- 1900–1924 Arts and Crafts and Art Nouveau

- 1920–1950 Plywood Furniture

- 1945–2000 Organic Modern

AMERICA

- 1900–1924 Arts and Crafts

- 1922–1930 Machine Age

- 1930–1945 Streamline

- 1940–1960 Organic Modern and Bauhaus

- 1982–2000 Post Modernism

Further Reading

Antique Trader Clocks Price Guide: Including All Types of Clocks - 17th Through 20th Century, edited by Kyle Husfloen and Mark Moran, published by KP Books (2002).

Antiques Trade Gazette, published weekly in the UK.

Bakelite Style: The Material of a Thousand Uses by Tessa Clark, published by Chartwell (2001).

Biscuit Tins: 1868-1939 by M.J. Franklin, published by New Cavendish Books (1999).

1000 Chairs by Charlotte Fiell and Peter Fiell, published by Taschen 25 (2005).

The Charlton Standard Catalogue of Wade Whimsical Collectables by Pat Murray, Published by Francis Joseph (1997).

Comprehensively Clarice Cliff: An Atlas of Over 2,000 Patterns, Shapes and Backstamps, by Greg Slater and Jonathan Brough, published by Thames & Hudson Ltd (2005).

The Complete Guide to 20th Century Antiques by Martin Miller, published by Carlton Books.

Decorative Arts 1950s by Charlotte and Peter Fiell, published by Taschen (2000).

Design of the 20th Century by Charlotte and Peter Fiell, published by Taschen (2000).

Encyclopaedia of British Pottery and Porcelain Marks by Geoffrey A. Godden, published by Hutchinson (1968).

Michael Hogben' s A–Z of Antiques and Auctions by Michael Hogben, published by New Holland (2006).

Mid-Century Modern: Furniture of the 1950s, by Cara Greenberg, Three Rivers Press (1995).

Miller's: 20th Century Design Price Guide by Paul Rennie, published by Mitchell Beazley (2003).

Miller's Collectables Price Guide 2007 edited by Jonty Hearnden and Katherine Higgins, published by Mitchell Beazley (2006).

Miller's: Collecting Furniture: The Fact at Your Fingertips by Christopher Payne, published by Mitchell Beazley (1998).

Miller's: Collecting Modern Design by Sally Hoban, published by Mitchell Beazely (2000).

One Hundred Years of Collectable Jewellery, 1850-1950: An Identification and Value Guide, by Lillian Baker and R.E.

Paperweights of the 19th and 20th Centuries: A Collector's Guide (Miller's Collecting Guides), by Anne Metcalfe, published by Collector Books (1978).

Poole Pottery edited by Leslie Hayward and Paul Atterbury, published by Richard Dennis (1999).

Sourcebook of Modern Furniture, Third Edition, by Jerryll Habegger and Joseph H. Osman, Published by W. W. Norton & Company (2005).

Treen for the Table, by Jonathan Levi and Robert Young, published by Antique Collectors' Club Ltd (1998).

Troika Ceramics of Cornwall by George and Wendy Perrott, published by Gemini Publications Ltd (2003).

Vintage Luggage: A Case Study, by Helenka Gulshan, published by Philip Wilson Publishers Ltd (2001).

INDEX

Page numbers in *italics* refer to illustrations

Abram Games 18
Adams, Barbara Linley 30
Adams, Harvey 29
animals: Black Forest 87
antiques:
  buying and selling 10
  damaged 11-12
Antiques and Collectibles 9
antiques fairs 10, *10*
Antiques Info 9
Arad, Ron 77
Art Deco 36
  bedroom suites 32, *32*
  furniture 92
  glassware 17, *17*
  mantle clocks 84
  marine paintings 50
  nursery ware 70
  pin cushion dolls 72
  powder compacts 41
  radios 54
  tureens 55
  wall mirrors 107, *107*
Art Nouveau 21
Arts & Crafts 36, 92
ashtrays: trench art 24
Attwell, Mabel Lucie 70
auction houses 10-11, *11*
  glossary 116
Avon scent bottles 106, *106*

Baccarat: paperweights 45
Baden-Powell, Robert
  Stevenson Smyth 19
badges:
  Boy Scout 19, *19*
  Festival of Britain 18
Baekeland, L.H. 54
Bailey, Barbara Vernon 70
Bailey, Lorna 112
Bakelite 54, *54*
Bamberg Metallwerkstätten 91
bamboo furniture 40, *40*
Bang, Michael 61
Barbie dolls 58
barge ware 100, *100*
Barton, Thomas 48
baskets: garden 20
Bateman, Hester: silver 31, *31*
Battersea: enamels 15
Bauhaus 91
Baxter, Geoffrey 61, 114
Bay ceramics 47

Beanie Babies 96, *96*
bedroom suites: Art Deco 32, *32*
Belleek 29
Berliner Metallgewerbe Joseph
  Müller 91
Beswick 57
Betts, J. 56
Bilston, Staffordshire 15
Birmingham: enamels 15
biscuit tins 18, 23, *23*
Bloomsbury: books 59
BMW 80
bookmarks: Stevengraph 44
books:
  Boy Scout 19
  'modern first-edition 59, *59*
Boy Scout memorabilia 19, *19*
Brando, Marlon 52
brassware: trench art *9*
Brauer, Otto 61
Braun 85
Broadhurst Company: pottery by
  Kathie Winkle 83, *83*
bubble cars 80, *80*
bullet shells 24
Bulova 85
button hooks: trench art 24
buttons 90, *90*

car boot sales 10
cardboard cut-outs: life-size 88,
  88
caricatures: *Vanity Fair* 26
Carlton 93
Carnival glass 16, *16*
cars: bubble 80, *80*
'cartes de visite' 53
Cartier 84
cartoons: Suffragette 25
Casio 14
catalogue of collection 13
ceramics *see* porcelain and
  pottery
Chad Valley 56
chairs:
  Coalbrookdale 20
  Mies van der Rohe 91, *91*
  Victorian 21, *21*
Chanel, Coco 105
Chelsea 99
chests of drawers: Victorian 21
chiffoniers: Victorian 21
china *see* porcelain and pottery
Christie's 10
chromolithographs 23
cigarette cards 19
Clash 66
Clichy 45

Cliff, Clarice 43, *43*, 93, 110, 112
clocks:
  alarm 85, *85*
  carriage 35, *35*
  glossary 117
  mantle 84, *84*
Cluett, William Charles 50
Coalport 55, 63
coffers 22
Collect It 9
collections:
  advice 12-13
  buying and selling 10-11
  cataloguing 13
  ideas for 8-9
  starting 9-10
collectors' clubs 10
commission rates 10-11
Comolero, Paul 13
Conran, Terence 57, 77
Constantine, George Hamilton
  50
Cooper, Susie 93, 110, *110*, 112
Corgi toys 69
Coronation: biscuit tins 23
Costa 61
costume jewellery 105, *105*
cranberry glass 13
Crawford's 23
crested china 28, *28*
crocodile skin 95, *95*
Crown Derby 29, 99
Crown Devon 29, 57
cruet sets: novelty 93, *93*
Cruise, Tom 52
Cullingford 33
Cumming, R.H. Neville 50

Dade, Frederick 50
damage 11-12
Davidson, George 39
Day, Lucienne 36, 65
Day, Robin 65
Deakins, John 45
Dean & Son 56
Derby 29, 99
desks: Victorian 21
Devlin, Stuart: silver 82, *82*
Diana, Princess of Wales 15
Dickinson, David 13, 102
Dinky toys 69
Dior, Christian 105
Disney:
  cardboard cut-outs 88
  toys for McDonald's 62, *62*
Ditchfield, John 102, *102*
dolls:
  Barbie 58

Photographic credits

All photographs were taken by Carl Warren, with the exception of the following, which were taken by Alan Marshall: Pages 10, 25, 28, 40, 47, 52, 74, 80, 81, 94, 101.

Publisher's Acknowledgements
The Publisher would like to thank Bekki Cartwright and Eugene Tiernan (stand FO14), of Alfie's Antique Market, for their generosity in allowing us to photograph the gorgeous Art Deco bedside tables seen on page 30.

Author's Acknowledgements
I would like to thank Carl Warren for taking such excellent photographs. A big thanks also to all of the traders who kindly let us photograph their stock, especially Peggy Pacy-Smith from Bagham Barn Antiques Centre, in Canterbury, for the location shots. Thanks as well to the superb team at New Holland, and finally, to my wife, Lesley, for typing up endless hours of my dicta-phone tapes!